WESTERN WIND
EASTERN SHORE

The Johns Hopkins University Press, Baltimore, Maryland 21218
The Johns Hopkins University Press Ltd., London

Robert de Gast's other books include
The Lighthouses of the Chesapeake
and *The Oystermen of the Chesapeake.*

WESTERN WIND EASTERN SHORE

A Sailing Cruise around the Eastern Shore of Maryland, Delaware, and Virginia

Written and Photographed by Robert de Gast   Foreword by John Barth

The Johns Hopkins University Press, Baltimore, Maryland 21218
The Johns Hopkins University Press Ltd., London

Manufactured in the United States of America

Library of Congress Catalog Card Number   75-10924
ISBN 0-8018-1767-6

Library of Congress Cataloging in Publication data will be found on the last printed page of this book.

Portions of the chapters covering the ninth through the thirteenth days of the voyage have appeared in the August 1975 issue of *Sail* magazine.

For Makaria, Sabrina, and Justin

Contents

Robert de Gast is a Dutch-born photographer, writer, and sailor who free-lances out of Baltimore and sails out of Annapolis, the Marblehead of Chesapeake Bay. In May 1974, he did a simple, delightful thing which no one seems to have thought of doing before, at least for the record: mostly alone, mostly under sail, he circumnavigated the Delmarva Peninsula, that shrimp-shaped entity (comprising Virginia's Accomack and Northampton counties, Maryland's Eastern Shore, and nearly the entire state of Delaware) which swims north toward Pennsylvania with its feet in the Chesapeake and the Atlantic on its back. Up from the Bay Bridge, through the Chesapeake and Delaware Canal, down Delaware Bay he sailed, poking into rivers, creeks, and byways on his way; then inside the skinny barrier islands along Delmarva's Atlantic shore (a route almost virgin to the cruising sailor), around Cape Charles, and up Pocomoke and Tangier sounds to his starting place, duly nosing into the Pocomoke River, the Little and Great Choptanks, the Tred Avon, the Wye, the Miles—most of the major estuaries and a few of the major creeks, big as rivers themselves, of the inexhaustible Eastern Shore.

Bertrand Russell observed about coastlines generally that their length can be measured only by ignoring enough actuality: coves, points, rocks, grains of sand. De Gast found this wistfully true of his twenty-four day circuit of Delmarva: the whole period would not have done justice to the Choptank alone, or the Wicomico, or the Nanticoke, not to mention the Wye, the Chester, the Sassafras. But he rediscovered the improbable Smyrna, the cypressed, tuckahoed, magical Pocomoke....

Any competent, imaginative sailor with a shoal-draft boat and three weeks on his hands might do as

Foreword by John Barth

much—must surely long to, once he reads this book. What Robert de Gast brought to the voyage (in addition to his delicate eye and lens, which need another paragraph) was the knowledgeability that makes his earlier photo-essays, *The Oystermen of the Chesapeake* and *The Lighthouses of the Chesapeake*, as delightful to those who know his subject intimately as to those who don't. Having mastered English *second*, he hears its tidewater dialect perhaps more accurately than we who grew up with it in our ears. He has done the requisite regional-historical homework; wears it lightly; invokes it aptly and unsentimentally. This voyager, like this voyage, is quiet, able, self-effacing.

He is seldom to be seen, for example, in the photographs which illuminate his text; neither is his shapely Olin Stephens sloop, *Slick Ca'm*. Nor are any human beings at all. These were among the first of a series of tactful artistic decisions—and surely the hardest for a sailor who loves his boat and a photographer who relishes people—following upon what I take to have been his working premise: that having essayed the oystermen and the lighthouses of the Eastern Shore, he would bring home this time, from this voyage, the place itself.

Properly, therefore, he works in black and white; that is, in infinite shades of gray. To the eye, the Eastern Shore is strictly, beautifully *monotonous*, especially those endless lowlands which, as a Netherlander himself, de Gast responds to with particular sensitivity. To Dutchmen, Eastern Shoremen, and shoal-draft sailors, the boundary between land and sea is never prominent and always negotiable; their world, as Jorge Borges remarked of the Spanish landscape, has few things in it, and so each thing exists with peculiar substantiveness. It is a world of such ubiquitous horizontality—sand bars, mud flats, the

360° horizon itself—that any verticals in it are more or less startling, interesting, even important, *ipso facto:* a mast; a piling; a heron's legs; loblolly pine trunks; the separate reeds of spartina grass. Even the surface of the water (everywhere!) is prevailingly "slick calm," at least in the pictures: Days One, Six, and Nineteen, when the seas got too vertical for photography, properly belong to the open-water passages of the voyage and text, not to the essence of either.

Mirrored in that calm, and in the tranquil lens and log of Robert de Gast, every low landfall is a Rorschach image: imposing nothing, evoking whatever the viewer, or voyager, brings to it. The skipper of *Slick Ca'm* brought more than most tidewater travelers, and more than any photographer so far, to his charming one-way round trip: neither a sea saga nor a soul-search nor a cruising guide nor a travelogue nor a coffee-table picture book, but a calm circumspection of the Eastern Shore.

This book is based on a log I kept and photographs I made during a twenty-four day circumnavigation of the Eastern Shore, the famed Delmarva Peninsula. Woven throughout the events of those days are stories about some of the places I visited and tales about historical incidents I never witnessed. The book is not a cruising guide, although it might be helpful to sailors contemplating a similar journey; nor is it a history or description of the Eastern Shore, which still awaits a definitive and scholarly accounting. Rather, it is an eclectic collection of remembered sights and sounds that focuses mainly on the edge of the Shore—the sailing route.

It was my intention to sail as close to the land as my shallow-draft boat could get, whenever possible weaving inside through cuts and channels, to poke up as many rivers and creeks as I had time for, and to photograph my environment as seen from the water. In some ways those were limiting requirements: often I wanted to be closer or to make my photographs from a different angle than could be achieved from where my boat could take me. But in another way this self-imposed restriction was liberating. The photographs became quick sketches, instant visual impressions—snapshots, if you will. I made all the photographs from the cockpit of my little sloop, usually while under way, with my foot on the tiller and my hand on the camera.

Some of the photographs reproduced here are intentionally small to help convey my feeling about the Eastern Shore's environment. The Shore is distinguished by a quiet, insinuating beauty, rather than by grandiose and overwhelming scenery. And admittedly, many of the scenes and activities the Shore is famous for cannot be photographed from the water. Nor did I choose the photographs to illustrate the text. They are intended to combine with the text, to give the reader my impressions of some of the land- and seascapes I encountered that seemed to me to convey the essence of the edge of the Shore.

There are a number of people I would like to thank: my wife, Evelyn Chisolm de Gast, for encouraging me to write; David Ashton, the designer of the book, for making it so handsome; John Barth and Jack Goellner, for their enthusiasm and support; and Henry Jarrett, my editor, for generous and skilled help in shaping the manuscript. Finally, I want to thank all the wonderfully hospitable people, some whose names I'll never know, whom I met on the edge of the Shore and who helped make my twenty-four days of circling and savoring their world among the most interesting and most enjoyable times I have ever spent.

Preface

The Eastern Shore—or, simply, the Shore—is a narrow, 135-mile-long peninsula bordered on one side by the Chesapeake Bay and on the other by Delaware Bay and the Atlantic Ocean. The *Encyclopaedia Britannica* does not dignify it with an entry; most dictionaries resolutely refuse to capitalize the two words; it is a designation without official geographic standing yet one of the best-known regional names in the United States, instantly recognized and identified, the way the Outer Banks are understood to be on the North Carolina coast.

It has been called the Eastern Shore since the Jamestown colonists first looked across the Chesapeake to its opposite shore. Captain John Smith began his account of his exploration of the Chesapeake in 1608 with the entry, "we crossed the bay to the eastern shore." The words were capitalized later in the seventeenth century, an unofficial practice that remains to this day.

The peninsula, occasionally called Delmarva—a word derived from the initial letters of portions of the states that it comprises (Delaware, Maryland, and Virginia)—has a population of nearly a million, remarkably evenly distributed among its six thousand square miles. It includes almost the entire state of Delaware, nine counties of Maryland, and two counties of Virginia. The narrow isthmus in the north (through which the Chesapeake and Delaware Canal was dug) forms its northern boundary.

In geological terms, the Eastern Shore is not very old. Its present shape was created less than ten thousand years ago, when the glaciers of the most recent ice age melted and boulders and detritus from the Susquehanna River built up a great shoal next to what was to become Chesapeake Bay, the drowned valley of the mighty Susquehanna. Its shape, of course, is constantly changing. Wind and tide wash the shoreline away;

The Eastern Shore

islands slowly disappear and reappear; canals are dug; marshes are filled.

The land is flat and fertile, and water is omnipresent. It would be difficult to find a spot on the Eastern Shore that is more than ten miles from navigable water, even though the Shore measures fifty-five miles at its greatest width. Dozens of creeks and rivers penetrate the Shore on the Chesapeake side, some of which nearly make their way across the peninsula toward the Atlantic.

At the turn of the century, J. H. K. Shannahan, in a book called *Tales of Old Maryland*, extolled the natural productivity of the Shore in these words: "It is a sand-bar, but it is something more; it is a garden, and an orchard. Nature seemed unkind when she strewed this sand upon clay without stones; but she repented, clothed it all in verdure, made it yield almost every fruit, vegetable, and berry in profusion and of finest quality, filled even the swamps with cypress, cedar, and pine, stored the streams with fishes, filled the waters along the coasts with shell-fish, crustaceans, and valuable finny creatures, sent flocks of birds into fields and woods, and flights of wild fowl upon all the waters."

The economy of the Eastern Shore has always been based on farming and fishing, and many writers have been reminded of food when looking at the outline of the Shore. John Barth has likened it to a shrimp, Hulbert Footner to a bunch of grapes. One nautical writer referred to its filigreed shoreline as "the deckplan of an octopus." Landlubbers might, with odd propriety, be reminded of a chicken thigh: poultry production is now the largest business on the Shore.

But farming, especially truck farming, is still very important. The farms are for the most part small but intensely cultivated, with sweet po-

tatoes, vegetables, strawberries, tomatoes, and small fruits among the chief products. The lower Eastern Shore, with its longer growing season, has many nurseries. Many of the Shore's industries are agriculture-related, with vegetable-freezing plants and canneries dominating.

The fisheries, of course, made the Eastern Shore famous and, for a time, rich. Most of the watermen are occupied by oystering in the winter and crabbing in the summer. The watermen have often been described as close-mouthed, wary of strangers, and quick with their fists. In fact they are uncommonly resourceful, stubborn, and energetic. The negative description may simply have resulted from an encounter by city slickers with people who obstinately cling to notions of their own. As Footner pointed out, "It has always been easy come, easy go on the Shore, with all that that connotes both good and bad. Everybody may have enough without working himself to death. The waters are full of food; until recent years there was game for everybody also; the garden will produce two or three crops in a season. This has resulted in an easy-going character. After three centuries of easy living, the Eastern Shore has established a tradition of the good life which insists on superior eating and drinking, leisure, sport and sociability. They are the greatest visitors and gossips in the nation. Hardship may be good for the character; ease develops the personality."

The first settlers were Englishmen. Few "foreigners" settled on the Shore. Its geographical isolation produced a fierce independence in its inhabitants. (More than once the Eastern Shore tried to make itself a separate state.) It was a place to go to, and stay; it didn't lend itself to passing through. Language and customs remained unchanged for centuries in some areas. Even today, the knowledgeable linguist can find traces of Elizabethan speech among the watermen, especially those who live on the more isolated islands.

The isolation was probably less pronounced in the early days, when people and goods were transported by water. Communication on the heavily timbered peninsula was only possible via boats, and waterfront sites were an economic necessity. In most areas on the Shore, the creeks and rivers were deep, and large ships could easily be accommodated. Shipbuilding became an important industry, helped no little by the ready availability of lumber for making masts, frames, and planking. But within two hundred years of the first settlement, the Eastern Shore had been nearly deforested and had become heavily cultivated. By 1815, the rivers and creeks were so silted up that many harbors became unusable for the ever larger and deeper draft ships. The channels

to the ports of Baltimore and Philadelphia allowed ships to sail farther inland, bypassing the Shore on both sides.

A travel story in *Harper's* a hundred years ago emphasized this isolation. "One still finds here the easy-going old-time life, the broad hospitality of our forefathers, the careless air of ancient gentility, just tempered by an aristocratic exclusiveness. So the peninsula lies winking at the hurly-burly of modern progress."

The numerous Indian names on the Shore are a constant reminder of the original inhabitants. Captain John Smith described his first meeting with Indians on the Eastern Shore in this way: "The first people we saw were two grim and stout Salvages upon Cape Charles, with long poles like javelings, headed with bone; they boldly demanded what we were, and what we would; but after many circumstances they seemed very

kinde, and directed us to Accowmack, the habitation of their werowance, where we were kindly treated. This King was the comeliest, most proper, civill Salvage we encountered. His country is a pleasant fertile clay soil, some small creeks; good harbors....They spake the language of Powhatan, wherein they made such descriptions of the bay, isles, and rivers, that often gave us exceeding pleasure." The werowance, or king, was Debedeavon, for unknown reasons called the Laughing King of Accowmack. The site of Accowmack that Smith refers to is some thirty miles south of the present town of Accomac. Smith's visit signaled the beginning of the generally excellent relations between the Europeans and the Indians on the Eastern Shore, and for a long time official communications from the king of England to his colony in Jamestown would begin with "To our faithful subjects of ye Colonie of Virginia and ye Kingdom of Accowmack." Within two hundred years all that remained of the Indians was the wonderful names they had given the places around the Shore:

Matapeake, Choptank, Tuckahoe, Wicomico, Wetipquin, Chesconessex, Pungoteague, Nassawadox, Wachapreague.

The character of the Eastern Shore changed drastically after the Chesapeake Bay Bridge was built in 1952. Thousands of travelers crowded the highways in summer in search of the cooling breezes and sandy beaches along the Atlantic. Property values skyrocketed, and tourism became a large industry. The lower Eastern Shore, Virginia's Northampton and Accomack counties (the name of the county is spelled with a *k* at the end, but the little town of Accomac, the county seat, survives without it), was initially spared this traffic until, in 1964, the Chesapeake Bay Bridge Tunnel was opened.

It is still possible to explore the Eastern Shore and experience the attraction of this flat and monotonous land in its pristine state. The best time would be in the spring or fall. And the best way would be by boat—by sailboat, as the first settlers had explored it.

I first saw the Eastern Shore more than a dozen years ago from the window of an airplane on a flight from Baltimore to New York. Once over Chesapeake Bay, the pilot banked his plane to arrive at the proper heading for La Guardia Airport. In the intense early morning light I saw what seemed like a never-ending succession of bright patches of water, only occasionally interrupted by the dark outlines of the land. I later found that I had seen Eastern Bay and the Miles River, a tiny, tantalizing portion of the Delmarva Peninsula.

Circumnavigating the Eastern Shore in a sailboat was an idea I began to entertain some years later. Studying charts in the winter is a fairly common activity among weatherbound and frustrated sailors. I was no exception. Although I was born in the Netherlands, a country dominated by water and the inescapable evidence of a great maritime heritage, I had not learned to sail until I came to live in the

Chesapeake area in the early 1960s. Since then I had sailed frequently, in a variety of boats, to many parts of the bay from my base in Annapolis. The Eastern Shore's rivers and creeks were most often the destinations for my weekend sojourns.

Dreaming of owning my own boat, and of possible voyages to places I had never been, I began poring over charts of the other side of the Eastern Shore, the Atlantic Ocean side. And slowly I began planning a journey *around* the Shore, through the Chesapeake and Delaware Canal, down Delaware Bay to Cape Henlopen, and then through the marshes behind the barrier islands along the Atlantic coast down to Cape Charles and back up through the more familiar waters of the Chesapeake Bay.

The charts indicated there was at least the possibility of such a voyage. But *A Cruising Guide to the Chesapeake* was not so encouraging. "There is an

Getting Ready

inside route that winds through bays and waterways behind the barrier beaches, and sometime in the future it may be navigable for cruising boats. For the present, however, it is too shallow and crossed by too many fixed bridges...." But, tantalizingly, the *Guide* went on, "It could be an interesting trip in a canoe, or a rowboat, or even a small outboard." I was hooked. I was going to try it in a sailboat. But first I had to find a sailboat.

I scoured the classified advertisements in the newspapers and talked to yacht brokers. The boat could not have a mast higher than about thirty feet and should not draw more than three feet. The first restriction related to the fixed bridges; most of them were about thirty-five feet above high water. The second was dictated by the depths indicated on my charts; most of the places I wanted to get through or to showed only three- or four-foot depths. And there was, of course, a third restriction—money. My dream boat just couldn't cost a whole lot of money.

Fortunately, the first two restrictions dictated a boat twenty to twenty-four feet in length; this imposed a kind of ceiling on the probable price. Even so, I became quickly convinced that I had to start looking for a boat that was in less than excellent shape if I were to afford one at all.

At last, in the spring of 1973, I found a twenty-two-foot keel-centerboard sloop in a marina on Kent Island, at the other end of the Chesapeake Bay Bridge from Annapolis. She belonged to a class called Sailmaster 22, and had been designed by Sparkman and Stephens, one of America's most famous and most successful naval architectural firms. She had been built in Holland some twelve years earlier just a few miles from the place where I was born. We were well suited to each other from the start.

It was obvious that she hadn't been loved in a long time. The bilges were filled with water to a point several inches above the cabin floor; somewhere in her past she had been attacked with a disk sander that had left mean scars and gashes on her mahogany trim. When she was last varnished it must have been done in a rainstorm, judging from the pitted, uneven surfaces. Her sails and rigging were in dire need of repair. Her fiberglass hull looked as if it had been rubbing against stone jetties for years. But I thought she was beautiful. Her neglected condition couldn't hide her lines, the traditional Dutch craftsmanship, the oversized fittings, the abundance of wood on and below deck, the potentially beautiful Sitka spruce spars, and the carefully thought-out layout. Besides, she was inexpensive.

E. B. White, in *The Sea and the Wind That Blows*, wrote: "If a man must be obsessed by something, I suppose a boat is as good as anything, perhaps a bit better than most. A small sailing craft is not only beautiful, it is seductive and full of strange promise and the hint of trouble. If it happens to be an auxiliary cruising boat, it is without question the most compact and ingenious arrangement for living ever devised by the restless mind of man—a home that is stable without being stationary, shaped less like a box than like a fish or a bird or a girl, and in which the homeowner can remove his daily affairs from shore as far as he has the nerve to take them, close-hauled or running free—parlor, bedroom, and bath, suspended and alive."

My new obsession could sleep four people in great discomfort, two with ease, and it was positively palatial for one person. There was plenty of storage space in lockers, on shelves, and underneath the bunks. There was a separate lazarette aft of the cockpit, with a hidden outboard motor well. A small, six-horsepower outboard came with the boat, as did a broken bilge pump, a two-burner alcohol stove (but only one burner worked), five mildewed life jackets, an eight-pound Danforth anchor with nine feet of anchor line, a soiled and tattered United States ensign, and an absolutely accurate compass. The cabin was cozy and comfortable, and the galley, consisting of an icebox and a sink, was entirely adequate. A Wilcox-Crittenden head completed the facilities in the cabin.

After pumping most of the water out of the bilges, I sailed my boat across the bay to Mill Creek, near Annapolis, where I hoped to keep her. I was a little ashamed of my yacht's condition and was not too sure she could handle the ten-mile trip, but I was anxious to berth her someplace where I could work on her. I needn't have worried; she performed well during the three-hour

journey in a moderate breeze.

Certain benefits accrue to authors, but none could mean more than the one accorded me by the Willards. John and Vera Willard run a small boatyard on Mill Creek. Keeping a boat with them would be safe, convenient to my home in Baltimore, and quite possibly inexpensive, because they didn't pretend to run a marina but catered almost exclusively to workboats and their captains. I sailed into Mill Creek and tied up to one of their piers. The Willard yard didn't look any different from the way it might have looked at the turn of the century. A dozen oyster boats and several sailboats were tied to piers that flanked a tiny marine railway. Mrs. Willard came out on the dock, and I introduced myself and my boat. She said she was sorry, but she didn't have any slips left, and maybe I should try one of the marinas in Annapolis.

"I would rather keep her in a working yard than

in a marina," I countered.

There was a long pause. "What did you say your name was again?" she asked.

I told her.

"That rings a bell." Another long pause.

"Aren't you the man who did *The Oystermen of the Chesapeake?*"

I said I was.

"Well," Mrs. Willard said, "I got that book as a Christmas present last year, and you'll fit right in. We'll find a slip."

I had a place to keep my boat. I renamed her *Slick Ca'm,* which is the Eastern Shore waterman's pronounciation of "slick calm," a condition of mirror-smooth water, when, as he would say, there ain't neither wind.

Slowly the long restoration process began. During the summer I tackled only the immediate problems, those that would not interfere with my sailing: the shorted navigation lights, the leaking cockpit, and those parts and pieces that could be sanded and varnished without affecting the operation of the boat. I wasn't going to waste the sum-mer. Besides, I was getting to know her intimately and had a chance to ponder minor changes before making them.

Winter would see her final transformation. I sailed her as often as possible and found her fast, able, and forgiving. On the last day of November I sailed *Slick Ca'm* in freezing weather a few miles from her berth on Mill Creek to Whitehall Creek, where Fred Willard, the Willards' son, who also owns a boatyard, hauled her out of the water and built a cradle so I could work on the hull during the winter.

Everything that could be removed, including the spars, I transported to the basement of my home in Baltimore. I would work on the hull in Annapolis on those weekends when it did not rain or snow. On inclement days I would work at home, stripping, sanding, varnishing, splicing, cleaning, and repairing.

By the middle of April she was back together, as good as new, and in some ways better. A few days later, her bottom was painted, and she was re-launched. I motored back to Mill Creek. John

Willard, a man of few words, gave the ultimate praise. "You really put a hurtin' on that boat," he said. I collected my washed and repaired sails from the sailmaker, and the following weekend, with the help of a fresh breeze, I held her "sea trials." She didn't leak, nothing broke, she looked glorious, and I had the satisfaction of easily outdistancing several sailboats ten feet longer than *Slick Ca'm.*

She was ready for the task I had had in mind for her all along: circumnavigating the Eastern Shore. Six months earlier I had chosen the month of May and vowed that nothing would interfere with my projected four-week cruise; I would simply be unavailable and incommunicado.

I wanted to make the voyage in the spring. It would not be too cold or too hot, I would be likely to have good breezes most of the time, and if I were lucky, the flies and mosquitoes on the Shore would not yet have hatched. Also, the tourists

would not have arrived yet either, and most yachtsmen, to their great loss, would not start cruising until June. I would have the place mostly to myself, and it would be a quiet trip. I chose the first of May. It happened to fall on a Wednesday, and that also pleased me. The boating activity on the bay on weekends would give me a false picture from the beginning. If I left during the middle of the week, I would be in or near the C. & D. Canal during the weekend and be away from the most concentrated boating activities.

The night before my departure I provisioned *Slick Ca'm* with groceries, clothing, gasoline, and alcohol fuel. I filled the water tank and put my twenty-four charts in sequence. I charged the battery one last time, then headed back to Baltimore for my last evening on land—at least, for some time. Early the next morning I drove the twenty-five miles back to Annapolis carrying my cameras, notebooks, and typewriter. A disc jockey on a local radio station mentioned that this was May Day. "Mayday" is also the international distress signal. I hoped it was not an omen.

Chesapeake Bay to Emory Creek It was nine in the morning, and a blustery day. "Small craft advisory is in effect," the radio announced. Was *Slick Ca'm* a small craft, or was "small" used to mean "incapable"? If the latter, I wouldn't have to worry about it: the boat at least was able. The water in Mill Creek was calm enough, although the leaves and branches of the trees were rustling. Force Six, I thought—a strong breeze, according to the Beaufort scale. In an earlier century, square-rigged ships would have struck their royals and flying jibs. I bent on my largest jib, the genoa. The wind effect at Force Six, according to Admiral Beaufort, forms large waves, extensive white foam crests, and probably some spray. Some spray for a square-rigger was a lot of spray for *Slick Ca'm*, but the admiral was describing conditions on the ocean, and I was only going out into the Chesapeake Bay. The sky was blue, the wind

out of the northwest, the tide flooding in an hour, giving me a one-knot push up the bay. I cast off my lines.

John Willard was working underneath a boat hauled up on the railway. He got up when he heard the sound of my outboard motor and walked over to the pier. He looked up at the sky and sniffed the air. "It's gonna be a late summer," he said. Then, as I slowly backed *Slick Ca'm* out of her slip, he called after me: "I envy you your trip. I'd like to see some of the places you're gonna see." I waved good-by and motored out of the creek.

Twenty minutes later, in Whitehall Bay, I changed my mind about the genoa jib. The mainsail alone would do nicely. For the first leg of my journey I intended to angle across the Chesapeake to the entrance to the Chester River, which would allow for a close reach all the way. I headed into the wind, turned off the engine, and started to

The First Day

raise the mainsail. But within seconds the force of the wind pushed *Slick Ca'm* broadside, and I couldn't raise the sail. I had already stowed the engine in the lazarette and didn't want to put it into the well again; after all, this was going to be a sailing voyage.

The wind and the waves were pushing us southeast. I crawled up on the foredeck and took the genoa off the jibstay, then hanked on the working jib, half the genoa's size. After hoisting the sail as tight as I could, I secured the halyard, made my way back to the cockpit, and trimmed the sheet. We were off—at hull speed. Now I had enough way on so that I could head into the wind and raise the mainsail, but that wasn't necessary. The speed limit of a displacement boat is easily determined: multiply the square root of the length of the hull at the waterline by 1.35, and that is as fast as the boat can go. The figure is always expressed in knots—nautical miles per hour. *Slick Ca'm* could do a bit over five knots—almost six miles per hour, and she was making that under the working jib. The mainsail never did go up the first day. The seas were five and six feet high; not a single fishing boat, yacht, or freighter was in sight. Three days earlier, on Sunday, I had stood on *Slick Ca'm*'s bow at the entrance to the Severn River and counted nearly four hundred sailboats. At the end of that first day, after sailing about thirty miles, I had not seen one boat.

At ten-thirty I was sailing under the Bay Bridge, properly known as the Governor William Preston Lane, Jr., Memorial Bridge. The bridge, a long-awaited highway link with the Eastern Shore, had been opened to traffic in the summer of 1952, nearly half a century after the possibility of building a bridge was first considered seriously.

A construction permit to build a bridge from

Millers Island, near Baltimore, to Tolchester Beach, then a popular resort on the Bay a few miles north of Rock Hall, had been issued in 1928, but the crash of 1929 made financing impossible. Twenty years later construction was finally begun, this time between Sandy Point and Kent Island, a distance of four miles, at the point where the Chesapeake is narrowest. The bridge curves so that the main channel meets it at right angles, a safety factor insisted on by the Army Corps of Engineers. The main span, of the suspension type, is 1,600 feet wide, and has a clearance of 186 feet. There are two ancillary spans, each 661 feet wide, but with a clearance of only 63 feet. The depth of water in the main channel is 54 feet. Some of the pilings supporting the bridge were sunk as low as 200 feet below the bottom of the bay; some of the steel reaches as high as 354 feet. The two-lane, $45-million bridge was opened to traffic on July 30, 1952.

When it was completed, the Bay Bridge was the largest continuous steel-over-water structure in the world. *Fortune* magazine, in a special article on the bridge, predicted that it would cut the crossing time by ferry, then half an hour—often with a wait of several hours on weekends—to less than ten minutes. The prophecy did not come true. Nearly two million vehicles crossed the bridge in 1953; twenty years later the total had reached nearly eight million. The waits became longer and longer, and weary travelers in the sultry summer heat longed for the return of the ferries.

In 1967 the Maryland State Roads Commission gave the go-ahead for the construction of a second, parallel span, opened in 1973. The new span, three lanes wide, cost nearly three times as much as the first. And there were still delays. Perhaps a boat was still the best way to cross the Chesapeake.

I plowed on, with the gunwales buried in the water, and at eleven-thirty I rounded Love Point lighthouse, or, rather, the foundation of the lighthouse that once stood there. The lacy screw-pile foundation was hard to spot until I was less than two miles away, even though visibility was excellent. Still under the working jib, I aimed for the wide mouth of the Chester River. The wind was now behind me, and *Slick Ca'm* began surfing in front of the waves. The temperature was in the low fifties; I had been wearing jeans and a sweater when I started out, and did not put on my foul-weather gear until it was too late. When we were on the wind, in the bay, *Slick Ca'm* hit a trough, slid down it, and hit the wave behind it. The force of the wind blew the top off the wave and doused me with spray. Then came the next trough, the slide, and more spray. By the time I reached the calmer waters of the Chester, I had already been soaking wet for an hour.

After I rounded Eastern Neck Island, at Hail Point (where the customs officials used to hail incoming ships two centuries earlier), the river curved northward again, and I was back on the wind. As I passed the entrance to Queenstown harbor, the wind increased. It was gusting to thirty-five miles an hour and on the edge of a gale. I was on a port tack and would have to come about soon. The shore was coming closer every second, and I had already passed the channel buoy. The chart showed I was in less than six feet of water. I put the helm over to change tacks. Nothing happened. The boat could not come about under her jib alone in this wind. I pushed the tiller in the opposite direction, jibed, and headed downwind and downriver. Queenstown, so blithely passed by two miles earlier, now seemed the ideal place to mull my situation over, dry off, square the boat away (the floor of the cabin was covered with charts and clothes I had not properly stowed), and make lunch.

Twenty minutes later I entered Queenstown harbor and promptly ran aground, but only momentarily. The boat's momentum helped push me through the shoal mud into slightly deeper water. Once inside the harbor I lowered the anchor, took down the jib, and tried to relax. I was on the Eastern Shore, but not exactly where I had planned to be. I had only been gone four hours and already I was soaking wet, had nearly run hard aground, was battling a gale. But I had crossed the bay in remarkable time, and I was warmed, at least in spirit, by the glow of an exciting sail.

The calm in the harbor was deceiving. After I had spent an hour at anchor in this protected cove, the weather outside did not look so bad. I had put on dry clothes and my foul-weather gear and boots, and I decided to head out again, under power, make my way up the Chester for a few more miles, and start looking for an anchorage for the night. When I hoisted the anchor up on deck, I also raised a cubic foot of mud that clung to the flukes. If I cleaned the anchor first, I would drift backward into the shoal again. I hauled the anchor, all eight pounds of it, adorned with at least twenty pounds of mud, and decided to worry about the mess later. As it turned out, the river cleaned the deck and the anchor for me. *Slick Ca'm* is a sea-kindly yacht, but not when she is under power. Her bow pounced down on the water, and the breaking waves cleaned the mud off in minutes. If the morning's run under sail had been wet and bouncy, the afternoon stretch under power proved to be more uncomfortable on the wide, choppy river.

I discovered that, although well stocked with food supplies, I had completely forgotten all the makings of breakfast—no milk, no bacon, no eggs. The *Coast Pilot*, a book of sailing directions, said that "some supplies could be obtained" at Centreville Landing, at the head of the Corsica River, a tributary of the Chester River. This suggested a grocery store, and I turned into the Corsica, the wind once again behind me. Under a warming sun I quickly forgot the plunging agony of the Chester. I turned off the engine and raised the jib again. On the way up the Corsica, an attractive river with only a few houses and farms discreetly tucked away along its banks, I noticed a small creek—Emory Creek, the chart said—that looked promising for an anchorage.

At five I tied up at the Centreville Landing wharf, a broken-down affair. Some teenagers directed me to the grocery store, several hundred yards up the road, where I bought milk and eggs, but not bacon. "No meats of any kind today," the proprietor said. I noticed that he added 10 percent to the marked prices. "Inflation, you know," he explained. I was looking forward to my eggs in the morning, and didn't argue. I walked back to the boat and sailed the few miles down the Corsica until I reached Emory Creek. I sailed until my centerboard touched bottom, then lowered anchor. A family of ducks, disturbed by my intrusion, paddled off with loud quacks, but a lone heron on the opposite shore, not a hundred feet away, seemed oblivious. I chipped some ice from my twenty-pound block, poured some vodka over it, took off my slickers and boots, and sat in the companionway contemplating this wonderfully quiet creek, its unruffled waters a soothing contrast to the wild Chester River just a few miles away.

In nearly ten hours of sailing I had covered twenty-nine miles and had not seen a single boat. I was safe and dry in a peaceful, pretty harbor. Maybe this wasn't such a crazy undertaking after all. But the discomforts of the day were not over

yet. After I had finished my cocktail, I gave serious thought to my dinner. Having decided on zucchini and corned beef, I tried to get my alcohol stove started. I had tested it, of course, before I left, and the one good burner had worked. But now the pressure wouldn't hold. I fiddled with it for half an hour, but finally had to settle for cold Vienna sausages and bread, and to do without coffee later. I didn't relish the thought of going without coffee or hot meals for the remainder of the journey, but I was too tired to worry about it.

It was dark now. I lit the anchor light and hoisted it up the jibstay. It really wasn't necessary; I certainly didn't expect to have company in this tiny, narrow creek, but it looked cozy anyway. I went down below. The cabin temperature was fifty-five degrees. I closed the hatch, unrolled my sleeping bag, and zipped myself in it. I was asleep in less than a minute.

Emory Creek to Worton Creek When I woke at sunrise the wind was still out of the north and seemed slowly beginning to shift toward the east. Breakfast consisted of cold cereal and an apple. No coffee, no eggs. I tried to repair the stove again but gave up when it became obvious that the pressure plunger was damaged beyond repair. Rather than go to Rock Hall, or Gratitude, as I had planned, I decided to head for Worton Creek, farther up the Chesapeake, where I knew there was a large marine hardware store and where the chances of getting the stove fixed seemed best Going up the Chester River to Chestertown was tempting, too, but I was already becoming impatient. I had not yet experienced the feeling of circumnavigating anything.

The Chester River is navigable for more than thirty-five miles, a good dozen miles beyond Chestertown. Hulbert Footner, author of *Rivers of the Eastern Shore*, writes: "After the Choptank, the Chester is the noblest of Eastern Shore rivers, more than a mile wide until after passing Deep Point, then averaging half a mile almost all the way to the head of navigation. Toward the mouth, it is confused with a maze of deep inlets, like the other rivers, but the shores of the upper reaches generally roll up unbroken."

The Chester was once a bustling river, and as little as fifty years ago steamboats regularly plied the river. The first steamboats on the Chester belonged to the Slaughter Line, which was organized in the 1840s and provided regular service from Baltimore to Chestertown. The trips to and from Chestertown to the western shore took the better part of the day; the steamers would dock and take on or discharge cargo and passengers at a half-dozen landings along the way. Peaches, especially, were an important cargo, and some summers more than

The Second Day

a million baskets were transported to the Baltimore markets. Settled in 1698, Chestertown was an important port long before the steamboats appeared, rivaling Annapolis and Oxford in trade and wealth. But its glories lasted only a short time. By 1760 Baltimore had overtaken Chestertown in tonnage shipped. Chestertown's beautiful houses of that period, however, have survived in nearly as great a number as those in Annapolis.

But I would not see them on this journey. By seven o'clock I was under way in a gentle breeze, with both the mainsail and the genoa jib up for the first time. It had turned colder during the night, and once out in the river I again donned my sweaters and foul-weather gear, even though the sail was not a wet one and the sky was clear; the foul-weather clothes served as perfect windbreakers. What I wouldn't have given for a hot cup of coffee!

Traffic on the Chester, besides pleasure craft

during the summer, now consists only of fishing boats and an occasional barge carrying petroleum products or grain. But a little after ten, after passing Love Point light again, I saw a boat, a sailboat, the first sign of nautical life in more than twenty-four hours. It looked like a thirty- or thirty-five-foot sloop. She was headed down the bay, too far away for me even to wave to. The wind kept shifting farther toward the east, and I had a fast and easy reach past Rock Hall and Gratitude. I stayed in the deeper water of the bay and avoided Swan Point Bar, a shallow three-mile-long oyster bed that had been the scene of one of the most decisive battles in the oyster wars that long troubled Maryland and Virginia.

In the 1880s several thousand sailing dredge boats ("drudgeboats," as the watermen aptly pronounce it) worked the waters of the bay. In 1885 more than fifteen million bushels of oysters were

raked and scraped off the Chesapeake's bottom. There were, and are, two kinds of oystermen: the drudgers, who use sailpower to scrape the dredge, and the tongers, who use long, scissorlike tongs to rake the oysters together and are permitted to use engines. Although drudging under power had been legal until 1865, it was outlawed that year as a conservation measure. The statute prohibiting drudging from powerboats remains essentially unchanged on the Maryland books. It is this law that is responsible for the presence, in Maryland waters, of the last commercial sailing fleet in the United States, the skipjacks, of which only about thirty now survive.

Shortly after the law was passed, bad feelings surfaced between the tongers and the drudgers. The drudgers, in their big, powerful sailboats, raked over the oyster bars that had been reserved for tongers, but the tongers could not repay in kind because the oyster beds reserved for the drudgers were too deep for their tools. In 1868 Maryland created an oyster navy to help keep the peace between the warring factions. By 1888, the oyster navy had acquired two steamers and twelve sailing patrol boats. There was a fair amount of chasing and some shooting between the law enforcers and the transgressors, but captures, casualties, and convictions were rare.

By 1888 the oyster business was booming, although competition was severe. In that year a number of drudge boats trespassed on the oyster bed of Swan Point; the drudgers rammed several tonging boats and indiscriminately fired rifles and shotguns at them. The tongers, unarmed and unharmed, first retreated and then retaliated. They mounted an old cannon on a point of land near Gratitude and, aided by the townspeople, most of them their neighbors, prepared to defend their legal rights. But during the night the drudgers came ashore and carried the cannon off. The show of force was successful, and the next day more than four hundred drudge boats were working the bar. The *Mary Compton*, one of the oyster navy's patrol boats, showed up and was promptly fired on. The patrol sloop's crew fired her muzzle-loading cannon once, but reloading took so long that the drudgers easily ran her off. By the time reinforcements arrived the drudgers had disappeared.

Several days later there were reports that the drudgers, now working in the mouth of the Chester River, had fired on the *Corsica*, one of the Baltimore–Chestertown steamers, perhaps on the assumption that she was a patrol boat. The oyster navy's flagship, the *Governor R. M. McLane*, was dispatched to the Chester and, finding the drudgers again illegally working a tonger's territory, called on the fleet to surrender. When the answer came in the form of a hail of bullets, the *McLane*'s captain started ramming the sailboats. Several surrendered, but most were able to flee. It was the last serious outbreak of violence between oystermen and the law, although minor scuffles still occur from time to time. The Maryland Code still states, in Section 702, that "it shall be unlawful for any captain or any person aboard a dredge boat to permit or have...any cannon, howitzer, or any piece of ordnance, rifle or musket."

Near Tolchester Beach, the channel for large vessels bound to and from the Chesapeake and Delaware Canal and Baltimore veers very close to shore. The wide expanse of the bay is deceptive here, for only near the shore is there deep water. I didn't particularly want to be in the channel, and so I sailed toward the middle of the bay. The fishermen take advantage of the shallow water here and set their seine nets. I spent the midday hours

dodging their buoys and stakes.

A few minutes after I dropped the hook it began to rain. I went down below, made a large pot of coffee on my stove, and picked up a copy of *Cruises—Mainly in the Bay of the Chesapeake*, written by two wealthy yachtsmen, George and Robert Barrie, around the turn of the century. They described my anchorage as it appeared to them then: "Worton's Creek is one of the snuggest anchorages imaginable. Seven feet can be carried up the creek to where it is completely landlocked. The wind can blow from any direction and one does not get a breath of it.... the banks are very high, and on the top of them are high trees. It would be a grand place to lie on a winter's night with a hard northwester blowing. One could sit peacefully near the cabin stove with no fear of dragging."

It sounded encouraging. I peered out of the hatch to check the Barries' description. Except for the marina, with more than three hundred boats at their moorings, the place hadn't changed a bit. I was still in civilization. After dinner—the eggs and zucchini I hadn't had the night before—I perused the charts. I had covered thirty-three miles that day, making sixty-two miles altogether. But I didn't feel like a circumnavigator: as the crow flies I was only twenty-two miles from Annapolis.

I went up on deck, took down the ensign, hoisted the anchor light, and let out another ten feet of anchor line. It was still raining softly. I closed the hatch, drank a toast of hot coffee to Art Willis, and went to sleep.

After a while I tired of this obstacle course and, since there was not a ship in sight, decided to hazard the channel. I had no sooner entered it when a large freighter appeared on the northern horizon. *Slick Ca'm* was making nearly five knots, and I assumed that the freighter was easily making three times that speed. In a very short time we had closed the gap between us, but I seemed on a perfectly safe course. I could see her port side and figured we would pass at least three hundred yards from each other. Then the freighter suddenly changed course and headed directly for me. A quick look at the chart showed a slight angle in the channel. Her pilot was in the right place, but I wasn't. I tacked with speed worthy of an America's Cup contender. We passed at 150 yards—a respectable distance, but too close for comfort. The freighter's bow waves were uncomfortably large, and although I easily rode the first one, the second one was very close behind it, and before my boat could recover from the first plunge, the second wave broke over my bow. The hatch was not closed, and most of the water found its way into the cabin. It was a great lesson.

I sailed to the nearest stout stake, tied up, mopped the water out of the cabin and the bilges, and made lunch—a sandwich and cold beer. At dawn the temperature had been forty degrees. Now, at noon, it had warmed to a sizzling forty-three degrees. I wondered why I had brought a bathing suit and short-sleeved shirts. And why I was drinking cold beer. What I needed now was a ski parka, gloves, and hot coffee. I remembered the broken stove. On to Worton Creek!

At three I sailed into Worton Creek's narrow entrance and near the end of the creek tied up alongside the gas dock of the marina. I took my alcohol stove under my arm and carried it inside the shop. The man behind the counter shook his head. "Parts for these things are hard to find. You should try Annapolis." I explained that I had just come from Annapolis, and that the only way I intended to get there again was by way of Cape Charles, and that in the meantime I didn't much

relish the idea of cold food three times a day for the next three or four weeks. My plea, I thought, was eloquent. I asked him to think of a way of possibly repairing the stove while I went next door to buy some bacon.

My appeal worked. When I returned with the bacon, another young man, whose name turned out to be Art Willis, stood smiling behind the counter. "Try this on for size," he said, pointing to the gleaming new pressure plunger attached to my stove. "I remembered having ordered it for a guy sometime ago. He never sails before June, so I'll get it replaced in time." I tried the stove, disbelieving. It worked as it never had before. I gave up my alternative plan for returning the bacon and making reservations at the nearest restaurant. I gladly paid the five dollars for the new part.

Art walked me back to *Slick Ca'm*. "Pretty boat," he said. "They don't make 'em like that any more. I heard you talk about your voyage back in the shop. Sounds like a great trip. Good luck!" I thanked him for his trouble and interest, untied *Slick Ca'm*, and headed down the creek to my anchorage for the night.

Worton Creek to Turner Creek I woke at daybreak to the sound of steady, heavy rain. I was annoyed and reluctant to leave the warmth and dryness of my sleeping bag. Hoping it would all go away, I took my time about getting up, making breakfast, and cleaning up. At eight I put on my boots and foul-weather clothes, and ventured on deck. There was plenty of rain but precious little wind. I hoisted the mainsail and genoa, raised and stowed the anchor, and slowly sailed out of Worton Creek into the Chesapeake. My next stop would be the Sassafras River, and it would be a slow beat the whole way. I steered by compass most of the time. Once in a while I could see the shoreline on my right, but most of the time I sailed in a pocket of visibility no more than a few hundred yards in diameter. Still, it was comfortable, much to my surprise. I had enjoyed a hearty breakfast, was wearing the proper clothes, and

had taken the trouble to lay compass courses earlier in the comfort of the cabin.

At noon I was at the wide mouth of the Sassafras. As I entered the river between the headlands, the sun came out, and simultaneously the rain stopped—for two minutes. Then there was a final shower, and although the sky still looked threatening in the west, the sun broke through the clouds in earnest. I gratefully took off my boots and slickers, hove to in the gentle breeze, and prepared my lunch.

In some quarters, cruising on the Chesapeake enjoys a bad reputation. Most people take their boats out on only Sunday afternoons, and if the wind and the weather aren't just right, they feel they've had another "typical" Chesapeake weekend. It is an undeserved reputation, for if you expose yourself and your boat to the vagaries of weather for only a little longer you are bound to

The Third Day

have a more varied, demanding, and therefore more satisfying experience. I had certainly had my share in the last few days: temperatures ranging from forty to sixty degrees, winds from zero to thirty-five miles or more per hour, sun, rain, and now again bright sunshine.

Hulbert Footner, in 1944, described the Sassafras this way: "As one travels northward, the land is always rising by imperceptible degrees, and for this reason the Sassafras is the most beautiful of Eastern Shore rivers and quite different in character from the streams farther south. The steep, wooded banks rise to a bench eighty feet above water level; it is only occasionally that one glimpses a sloping wheatfield behind a screen of trees. Each of the many inlets winds away to disappear mysteriously in the shadows of its lofty banks. The variety is endless. Each point, as you round it, reveals a green surprise. The course is like a succession of little land-locked lakes; you can never see far. The Sassafras is something special in rivers, yet few know it, even in Maryland."

His description holds true today, even the last sentence, for although yachting activity in the last thirty years has increased a hundredfold, most of the yachtsmen, who keep their boats at Georgetown, ten miles up the river, come from Delaware, New Jersey, and Pennsylvania, whose borders are not far away.

After lunch I continued toward Georgetown. I wanted to explore the river above the bridge, where it is navigable for another three miles. Georgetown is the yachting center of the upper Eastern Shore. Just below the bridge several marinas vie with each other for size and accommodations. Hundreds of powerboats and sailboats were berthed here. I tied up to one of the piers to buy two and a half gallons of gasoline. A

sign on one of the piers said Cream Puff Alley. The few people in evidence were all paid hands, scrubbing and polishing their employers' vessels. A carefully lettered sign announced that today's edition of the *Wall Street Journal* was available. This was not the Eastern Shore I was looking for. The pump attendant told me that the bridge had broken down the day before. It could neither open to allow boats to pass through nor support vehicles. He grumbled about the ten-mile detour he had had to make to get home. I grumbled about not being able to reach the head of navigation. I stowed the spare gas can, turned around, and sailed back down the lovely Sassafras.

The weather forecast was not very good either: northwest winds, twenty to thirty miles per hour, expected in the evening and all day tomorrow. I had been hoping to make the Chesapeake and Delaware Canal sometime the following day, and perhaps the closing of the bridge was just as well; I would find a snug spot for the night as close to the mouth of the Sassafras as possible. In a failing breeze (the proverbial stillness before the storm) I sailed toward the mouth of the river. At Ordinary Point I turned south and insinuated *Slick Ca'm*

into Turner Creek, a shallow, completely land-locked lagoon, difficult to enter.

It was near Turner Creek that Captain John Smith, during his second voyage of exploration of the Chesapeake in 1608, had been royally entertained by the Tockwogh Indian tribe. "Their men, women, and children," he wrote, "with dances, songs, fruits, furs, and what they had, kindly welcomed us, spreading mats for us to sit on, stretching their best abilities to express their loves."

At six I was inside the creek and anchored. I had tried exploring the length of the creek, nearly one mile, but it shoaled rapidly, and I abandoned the idea. I made dinner and measured my progress. Only twenty-two miles. After dinner I sat in the cockpit and caught the last of the warm sunshine. Just before sunset the clouds moved in, the wind piped up as predicted, and the temperature fell rapidly. I got a sweater from below and stayed up on deck until it was pitch dark. The placid lagoon now showed small wavelets. I hoisted the anchor light, checked whether my anchor was holding well, closed the cabin hatch, and turned in for the night.

Turner Creek to Chesapeake and Delaware Canal
A kind of motion that didn't seem right woke me out of a deep sleep. *Slick Ca'm* was not riding the waves easily, and the waves were making an unusual, slapping sound. I stuck my head out of the hatch. There was a full moon. Even in this wonderfully protected anchorage I could tell that it was really blowing outside. Several of the fishing boats on moorings nearby were pointing in a different direction from mine. They were lying into the wind, whereas my stern was facing it. Barely awake, I needed several minutes to figure out what was going on. The strong wind had blown a lot of water out of the creek, and this, combined with the low spring tide, meant that with the centerboard down we were stuck in the mud. I climbed into the cockpit and raised the board. *Slick Ca'm* floated free and headed briskly into the wind. I let out another twenty feet of line and quickly crawled back into my warm sleeping bag. The temperature outside was near freezing.

At sunrise, when I woke again, I could hear the wind howling through the rigging. Its velocity had increased. I reached for my radio without leaving the warmth of my berth. "Small craft advisory, with strong, gusty winds from the northwest." I debated staying in and letting the breeze blow itself out. But after cereal, bacon and eggs, and coffee I felt ready to face the day. I dressed for the occasion: boots, foul-weather gear, sou'wester. It was becoming my uniform.

I carefully motored out of the creek. The channel was much shallower than it had been the day before, and so was easier to see and follow. I was out in the mouth of the Sassafras, and the wind was blowing straight into it. It was not going to be easy to sail out of it. That would only be fair, I thought. After all, getting in had been easy. I raised the

The Fourth Day

mainsail, cranked a reef in her, then hoisted the working jib. I hauled in the sheets, the wind filled the sails, and *Slick Ca'm* lay over on her side and plowed into the waves, rail in the water.

The few miles to be covered between my starting point and Turkey Point occupied most of the morning. At the mouth of the river the waves were higher—fully six feet. I thought how pleasant it would be to run back to Turner Creek before this wind. But *Slick Ca'm* was taking it well, though slowly, even though her skipper wasn't. Everything was drenched. The ice-cold spray lashed across my face each time we plunged into a trough. I improvised a pair of gloves with some woolen socks, but this helped for only a few minutes.

Shortly before noon I was in the Elk River and in the lee of the high bluffs at Turkey Point. I inched toward shore until the centerboard touched the bottom and dropped the anchor

twenty feet from the beach. I went down below to warm up, dry out, and make lunch. An hour later I was under way again. I shook out the reef and, protected now by the high land on my port, sailed on a close reach toward the entrance of the Chesapeake and Delaware Canal.

It had been a long, tiring, agonizingly slow morning. But now I was making progress again. When I reached the entrance to the canal, at Welch Point, I took down my sails and stuck the outboard back into its well. The Code of Federal Regulations, Title 33, paragraph 207.100, subsection (s), states very clearly: "Sailboats. Transiting the canal by vessels under sail will not be permitted." This was disappointing, for I could really have made time under sail; the wind was nearly behind us now at more than twenty knots. I briefly considered blithely sailing on. There were no patrol boats in sight, but I knew that closed-

21 Miles

circuit TV cameras at both ends of the canal were being monitored by the Corps of Engineers. So I obeyed the law.

The waters of the Chesapeake and Delaware bays are here separated by only fourteen miles. As early as 1654, Johan Rising, the Swedish governor of what is now Delaware, proposed a canal to connect both bays. In 1661 the idea was proposed again by Augustine Herman, sometime Dutch envoy from New Amsterdam to St. Mary's, in Maryland. (In the meantime the Dutch had wrested the colony from the Swedes.) Herman was halfway through a ten-year project to map Maryland and the rest of the Eastern Shore, and he was well aware of the close proximity of the two bays.

More than a hundred years passed, however, before survey teams began their initial work, and it was not until 1804 that digging was actually started. The Chesapeake and Delaware Canal Company had been formed in 1799, but lack of funds halted digging in 1806. Work was eventually resumed in 1823, and in 1829 the canal was opened. It was not much of a canal, compared with the present one. Although the canal itself was ten feet deep and had a water-line width of sixty-six feet and a bottom width of thirty-six feet, four locks of much smaller dimensions had to be negotiated. The locks were only twenty-two feet wide and could not accommodate vessels drawing more than seven feet. But the canal was an immediate success. Within two years tolls were averaging $2,600 a week, mostly from coal and lumber barges. As larger ships were built, the locks were enlarged—to 220-foot lengths and 24-foot widths—but they were still too restricting.

In 1906 Theodore Roosevelt appointed a commission to study the merits of a "free and open waterway to connect the Chesapeake and Delaware Bays"—in other words, a tidal canal, without locks. The commission reported favorably. In 1919 the federal government purchased the canal for $2.5 million, and immediately spent nearly $11 million to widen the canal to ninety feet, deepen it to twelve feet, and remove the locks. Within a decade, shipping volume reached one million tons, and the canal again became inadequate. Between 1935 and 1938 the canal was widened and deepened again. That was not enough, either. In the late 1950s and the early 1960s, more than $100 million was spent to bring the canal to its current dimensions—450 feet wide and 35 feet deep—and to construct several high bridges. This may have been the last enlargement, for the approaches from both the Chesapeake and Delaware bays cannot accommodate ships drawing much over forty feet.

This was Saturday, and a number of small pleasure craft, nearly all motorboats, were using the canal. I tied up at Shaefer's Canal House, a marina and restaurant underneath the bridge at Chesapeake City, and decided to have dinner there before venturing into Delaware Bay. It was now necessary for me to take a shower before I could participate in "society" again. A helpful attendant on the dock directed me to the ladies' room; the shower in the men's room was not working. A shower was the only thing I really missed on *Slick Ca'm;* it was still too cold to swim. I stayed underneath the shower for fifteen minutes and began to understand people who try to cram a shower into a tiny boat. When I emerged from the ladies' room I was confronted by the most agonized stare I have ever seen. A young man, seated in his parked car a few feet from the door, alternately looked at me and the sign on the door I had just come through. I judged him to be in his late teens. I grinned and

winked at him conspiratorially.

I stayed tied to the pier until dinnertime, but I didn't get much rest. Instead, I had to scramble about to rearrange my lines and fenders after the wake of the first large ship had rubbed my topsides nearly bare. After dining on a delicious rockfish stuffed with crabmeat, while watching a dozen or so huge ships sail by the restaurant's windows, I returned to the dock.

Just before boarding *Slick Ca'm* I saw a sailboat, with masts bare, silently glide by. She carried no lights. The current was carrying her toward the Chesapeake at nearly two knots. A voice called out, "Anybody have any gas over there?" I advised the caller to anchor and promised I would get over to him. I started my engine and went in pursuit of the ghost ship, which I overtook in a few minutes; she had anchored half a mile past the bridge. I headed into the current and tied up alongside the forty-foot sloop. Her skipper had run out of gas some miles before the bridge and had coasted with the current. Without power, he could not maneuver his boat close to the dock. There was no way I could tow her back to the marina against the current. So one of the crew members went back with me, armed with a small tank that could hold enough gas to get the boat's engine started and get her back to the dock.

When we reached Shaefer's dock, the pumps were closed. It was nearly ten o'clock. A man on the dock offered the stranded mariner some gasoline from his car and a hose to siphon it out with. He wouldn't accept payment. It was typical of the self-effacing helpfulness I was later to experience many times on my journey.

As soon as the grateful young sailor had his engine working again, I motored back toward the bridge, then turned into the anchorage basin on the Eastern Shore side of the canal. Here I would be totally sheltered from the wakes of passing ships. Only one sailboat shared the huge basin with me. I went to the farthest end, lowered anchor, and poured myself a nightcap to celebrate the rescue. I now had the feeling—finally—that I was actually going around the Eastern Shore. Tomorrow I would be in the Delaware River.

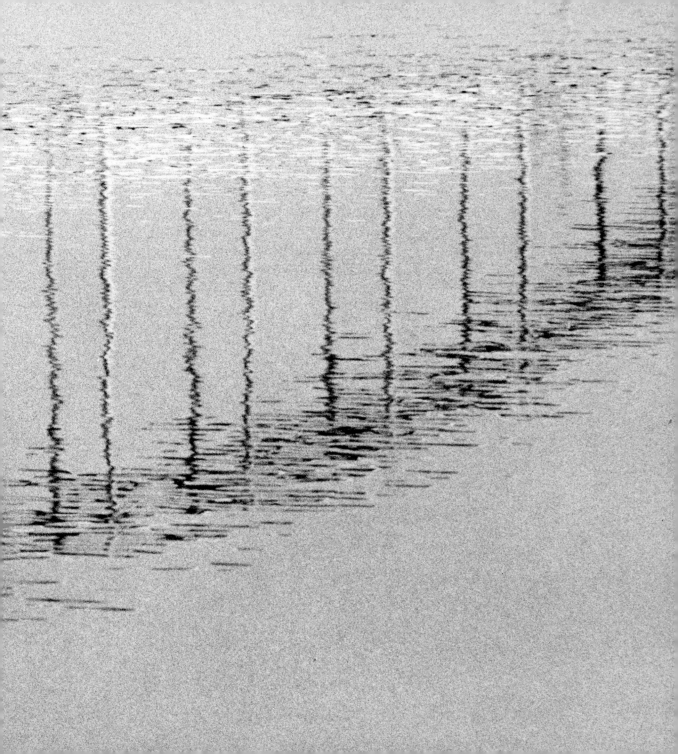

Chesapeake and Delaware Canal to Smyrna River I woke at sunrise; it was getting to be a habit. It was cold—thirty-four degrees in the cabin—but the skies were clear, and there was the hint of a breeze. I still had to motor nine miles before I'd be out of the canal and into the Delaware. After a leisurely Sunday breakfast, I perused the *Tidal Current Tables*, an annual listing daily predictions of the times of slack water and the times and velocity of maximum flood and ebb currents. In two hours the favorable tide would be over and slack water would begin. If I hurried, I could be out of the canal by then. I hastily cleaned up and by eight o'clock I was on my way again. After dodging a few freighters and some tugs with barges, I emerged from the canal at ten. I was on the Delaware River.

That hint of a breeze had not materialized, but I optimistically raised the main and genoa anyway.

One hour later I was still in sight of the jetties at the Reedy Point entrance to the canal. There was no breeze at all, and now the tidal current, flooding, was inexorably pushing me back. Reluctantly I lowered sail and started the engine again. Sunday brought no holiday for commercial traffic. Dozens of tankers and freighters made their way up and down the river. I stayed outside the shipping lanes, skirting the low and marshy western shore.

The Delaware has none of the gentleness of the Chesapeake. It is all business, and the hand of man is evident almost everywhere. With few harbors, plenty of shoals, and, when the wind is against the tide, steep and short seas, the Delaware is universally disliked. The *Cruising Guide*, referring to approaches to the Chesapeake, minces no words: "Yachtsmen may argue violently about the relative merits of the Chesapeake and the Coast of Maine; they may differ elo-

The Fifth Day

quently about the cruising merits of Long Island Sound compared to Narragansett Bay. But there is one body of water on which there is complete agreement; we haven't heard one dissenting voice—they all dislike it with varying degrees of eloquence according to their gifts of self-expression. We are speaking of Delaware Bay." I agree that this "body of water" does not offer pleasant sailing, but some of its fringes are strikingly beautiful, particularly the area around Smyrna River.

I reached the mouth of the Smyrna at mid-afternoon. I was low on gasoline, and since I had read in the *Coast Pilot* that at Flemings Landing, some three miles up the river, gasoline and some supplies were available, I headed there. But I had another reason for going up the Smyrna. In 1940 Joe Richards, a painter and illustrator, sailed a Friendship sloop, a small Maine coast fishing boat, from New York to Florida. Fifteen years

later he described his journey in a book which he named after his boat, *Princess–New York*. It became a classic about sailing small boats.

In July 1940, Richards found himself in Delaware Bay, harassed by high winds and choppy seas. "I searched the chart for a brief haven," he recounted. "There was a wrinkle on the chart, a tiny tributary of the Delaware called Smyrna River seven miles above Ship John Light, that might offer a comfortable anchorage before the wind and the tide started throwing things again...." Richards made his way into the narrow river. Here is how he described his feelings: "To be transported so suddenly from the hammering violence of the Delaware to this silence and this beauty made me wonder for a moment if I was alive.... To find this deep river, to be folded in the silence of this tall grass, to move without sound or wind or without grounding through the majesty of these towering, golden-green reeds when the

mind is tired and the body starved for sleep is an accident. As I held to the mast and saw the peaceful pastures, the motionless low hills, the quiet farmland between the thinning blades of the reeds, I knew I was dead or crazy."

In thirty-four years the landscape hadn't changed at all. I was a little sorry that I wasn't under sail, but with no wind and the current against me, I would never have made it even to the bridge. I had never been on such a meandering river. Never more than a hundred feet wide, and seldom with a stretch more than a hundred feet long, it seemed interminable. I became more and more concerned about my dwindling supply of gasoline. It might take days just to sail out of the river again, days waiting for the right combination of wind and tide.

Finally, around one more bend in the river, I saw a bridge ahead and, just before it, a disintegrating dock, a dilapidated shed, and the rusty remains of a small marine railway. This was the boatyard mentioned in the *Coast Pilot*. Three big crab boats were tied to some old pilings. Fifty feet beyond, at the bridge, the river narrowed between the sluiceheads. As I tied up to one of the boats,

my engine burned the last ounce of fuel, sputtered, and died. I disconnected the tank and retrieved it from the lazarette, then picked up my empty reserve tanks and, still hoping that gasoline would not be far away, walked across the fishing boats to shore. It was obvious that it had been years since anything had been built or repaired here. The only house in view was boarded up. I put the cans down and walked across the bridge.

A young man was fishing in the rushing current on the other side of the bridge. Long, blond hair spilled out from underneath his cap, which had a marlin embroidered on the front; there were several fishing tournament patches sewn to his overalls. He looked no more than twenty years old. Still convinced that gasoline was near, I asked him to direct me to a pump. He stood up and began giving the most elaborate and convoluted directions. It was obvious that I couldn't walk to wherever it was. He had been so engrossed in his fishing that he hadn't seen me sail up to the boats on the other side of the bridge. When he realized that I did not have a car, he shrugged and said, "Come on, I'll take you." Hidden behind a grove of trees was his car, a huge white Cadillac of uncertain vintage. The volume of the radio made conversation impossible during our ride. At the first gas station in the nearest town—ten miles later—I filled both of my tanks and his Cadillac's tank, too. I didn't know Cadillacs held so much fuel. He apologized for having a nearly empty tank but explained that he was out of work. In the face of his unemployment he had offered to drive me twenty miles without certainty of compensation. On our way back the radio again precluded conversation. Back on the bridge, I asked him about the river beyond it; according to the chart, it was navigable for another five miles or so. "Ain't seen a yacht here for years," he said. "Takes twenty-four hours' notice to get the bridge opened. Ain't nobody using it." I thanked him and carried the fuel back to *Slick Ca'm*. Then I headed down the river to find an anchorage for the night.

I anchored in one of the wider bends in the river, where I would have some room to swing. I lowered anchor in ten feet of water and also raised the centerboard—it was high tide, and at low tide the water would only be four feet deep. I had traveled nearly thirty miles, not counting my automobile excursion, and I was in the most deserted and most desolate area in Delaware. Just before sundown a small skiff raced up the river. The skipper momentarily slowed down. "All right?" he asked. "All right," I replied. He went on and not once looked back. The laconic query expressed the concern that people on the water often show. A sailboat anchored in the middle of the Smyrna River looked like trouble. Two words were enough to verify that it wasn't.

It started to drizzle. Before going below to prepare dinner I hung the anchor light in the rigging. I didn't want the crab boats at the landing to plow into me if they went out before sunrise. "A collision at sea can ruin your entire day," the old saying goes. Or ruin your night, I thought. My first day on the Delaware hadn't been so bad. Perhaps in the morning I would have a sailing breeze. And I was delighted to have discovered the Smyrna. I turned out the light and went to sleep.

Smyrna River to Roosevelt Inlet The crab boats from Flemings Landing roared past me long before sunrise, and their violent wake shook me out of my sleep. By the time I had jumped out of my sleeping bag and stuck my head out of the hatch, they had disappeared behind a bend in the river. I decided to get up anyway and watch the sunrise. It was a spectacular show. The weather was very cold, but the sky was clear, and it promised to be a lovely day. The only forecast I could hear on my radio was for the Chesapeake, but not the Delaware, Bay—unfortunately, as it turned out.

By seven I had finished breakfast, tidied up the cabin, washed down the deck, started the engine, and was under way. The current was against us and cut our speed to barely two knots. There was a spot on the chart that marked a two-foot shoal at the entrance to the river; I promptly found it and ran aground. I succeeded in pushing us off the soft mud patch with a long oar, and by eight I had left the quiet water of the Smyrna and had entered the Delaware, where the water was even quieter. No wind again, and the current against me. I headed for Ship John Shoal lighthouse, its sixty-foot-high tower an easy reference point. I would be bucking the tide until noon. I had spent some time earlier in the morning laying out compass courses in case I couldn't identify buoys or landmarks visually; it turned out to be time well spent. The sun disappeared behind fast-moving, low clouds. Now it looked as if I might get both wind and rain. I stayed as close as I could to the Delaware side of the bay. The water was still mirror-smooth, and I was becoming bored with motoring and with the Delaware, too. Lewes, near Cape Henlopen, was still about forty miles away. At Lewes I would go inside the Lewes and Rehoboth Canal, the first leg of the Inside Passage.

The Sixth Day

The traffic in the ship channel was heavy. There was also a lot of floating debris: logs, tree trunks, and planks. I didn't relish the thought of having to sail these waters at night. From time to time the sun peeked through the clouds and warmed me up for a few minutes. I kept sailing a course along the edge of the shoals to stay out of the way of the huge tankers and freighters. Several times my centerboard hit bottom. The hinged board acted like a depth-finder; when I heard it scrape I knew I had only two and a half feet of water before we would be hard ground.

Running aground, a frequent occurrence on this trip, was never the terrifying experience here that it can be in other places. In Maine, for example, hitting a rocky ledge can be catastrophic. The sandy and muddy bottoms of the Chesapeake and Delaware bays make running aground an incident—an inconvenience, at worst. In a small

boat like *Slick Ca'm* jumping overboard and pushing off was often the quickest solution.

Although bored, I was still grateful for the quiet water. I had had my share of high winds and seas. By ten I was out of the Delaware River and into the ever-widening waters of the bay. Having decided to go straight to Lewes, I now stopped skirting the curving shore and sailed down the middle of the bay toward its mouth.

Henry Hudson, the English navigator employed by the Dutch East India Company, is credited with discovering Delaware Bay on August 28, 1609. Hudson, sailing the *Half Moon*, was searching for a northwest passage to China and the Indies. Not having a small enough boat to take soundings, and reluctant to put his ship in jeopardy in the shallow uncharted waters of the bay, he did not waste any time exploring but instead sailed north to the river that still bears his name. A

49 Miles

year later Captain Samuel Argoll, from the new colony in Jamestown, sailed his *Discovery*, a small pinnace, to the entrance of the bay. He named the southern point Cape La Warre, after Lord de la Warre, who was then governor of Virginia. The cape is now called Henlopen, probably after Hindelopen, a small port in the Netherlands. In 1616 Cornelis Hendricksen, in the employ of the 'Staaten Generaal of the United Netherlands Provinces, explored the bay in *Onrust* ("Restless"), one of the first ships built in what is now the continental United States. Hendricksen reported that "he hath found the climate of the said Country very temperate, judging it to be as temperate as that of this country Holland."

I, too, found the climate much like that of Holland, where I had spent my boyhood years. But I certainly didn't think it temperate. When the tide turned, the breeze picked up. It was noon, and still only forty-five degrees. In a few minutes it began to drizzle. The shore, already difficult to distinguish because of distance, disappeared in the murk. When I nearly ran into a buoy which the chart showed to be ten degrees off my course, I realized that my always-accurate compass was being deflected. My radio and camera turned out to be the culprits. I stowed them both far from the compass.

The wind increased to about twenty-five knots. Now I could sail! I raised the main and the working jib, but after a few minutes I roller-reefed the main a few turns. I could just lay a straight course for Roosevelt Inlet, the entrance to the Inside Passage. The tide now helped my progress, but it set up one of the worst choppy seas I have ever experienced. Steep, six-foot waves crested in rapid succession and nullified any of the extra push I was getting from the tide. Each time *Slick Ca'm* plunged over a wave into a trough, spray flew back over the cabin into the cockpit. In minutes I was drenched. I had been wearing foul-weather gear and now reached down below for my boots. Already my socks were soaking wet. I skipped lunch. Each shuddering plunge and dose of drenching spray increased my determination to get out of Delaware Bay as soon as possible. With a little luck I could make it before sundown.

At six that evening I could see the Delaware shore again—first the breakwater at Cape Henlopen, then the water tower at Lewes, and finally a thin strip of beach. The chart showed the beach to be near Roosevelt Inlet, yet I still couldn't see the entrance. I spotted a small tugboat heading for the beach and followed in her path. In minutes I was within the outstretched arms of stone enclosing the inlet, and the waves were gone. I was out of Delaware Bay. I had never, in such a small boat, sailed as long and uncomfortably as I had that long afternoon. I made a sharp turn into the canal, lowered sail, and slowly drifted with the current toward the bridge at Lewes, anchoring two hundred yards from it. It was almost dark. My face, hands, and clothing were gritty with salt. I dried off and cleaned up as best I could. Then I went up on deck again and hung the anchor light in the rigging. The rain had stopped, but ominous-looking black clouds were now racing in from the north. I put chafing protectors around my anchor line and, too tired to make dinner, went below again and fell asleep immediately.

Roosevelt Inlet to Indian River Inlet I awoke in the dark with the knowledge that something was wrong. The cold front, as I found out later, had come through full force a little after midnight. My anchorage, fully exposed to the northwest, was no longer the haven it had seemed after I had come out of Delaware Bay. I had been aware, at least subliminally, that we had been going around in circles. The current would force us in one direction, and the wind, whenever it gusted up, would point us in another one. I was snug enough in the cabin. The anchor was down properly, it had plenty of scope, and I was, after all, in a canal, with the houses of Lewes bordering it on both sides. I opened the hatch and saw that I was ten feet from some pilings on the edge of the canal. We were obviously dragging anchor—and too fast for comfort. Yet I first put on pants and a sweater, for I did not know how much time I had before we would hit the pilings, and it was bitterly cold outside. It turned out to be a good idea, for I was on deck for nearly forty-five minutes.

First, I started the engine and slowly motored toward the anchor and away from the pilings. The wind was howling now. I hoisted the anchor aboard. Mud oozed from the flukes. I cursed my luck for not getting in early enough to make it to more protected water on the other side of the bridge. But the bridge opened only from six in the morning until seven at night, so the *Coast Pilot* said. I headed a little farther into the wind and dropped the anchor again. We were in ten feet of water. I let out thirty feet of line, then fifty. We were still dragging. One hundred feet, then one hundred and fifty—all I had. A slight shift of wind kept me in the middle of the channel, away from the piers on either side of the canal. Still we drifted slowly toward the bridge. If the bridge

The Seventh Day

should open now I could drift through it backwards. Using the engine at half throttle, and taking advantage of the frequent gusty wind shifts, I slowly began making arcs—this time on purpose.

In a few minutes the motion put me closer to the edge of the canal, so that I could grab one of the pilings—the same ones I had seen after waking up. It seemed simple. Grab the piling, tie up, and go back to sleep. But between the swift current and the wind it took another half an hour before I could maneuver *Slick Ca'm* between the pilings without damaging her. At one time I had six lines tied to various pilings. With two people it would have been a cinch. Finally *Slick Ca'm* was securely tied between four pilings.

Properly moored at last, I went back to my sleeping bag, in which it was now as cold as it was outside—thirty-five degrees. I pulled on a pair of woolen socks and fell asleep with my clothes on.

But at 7:00 A.M. I was awake again. My internal time clock had become synchronized with the movement of the sun. The wind had died down somewhat, but I decided to stay in Lewes until it calmed a bit further. My next stop would be Indian River Inlet, and I would have to cross the shallow waters of Rehoboth Bay. And with this northwester a lot of water would have been blown out of the bay. After breakfast, my first meal in twenty-four hours, I walked over to the bridge tender's office. The *Coast Pilot* was wrong; the bridge at Lewes has a tender on duty twenty-four hours a day. I sat in the warm office and told of my ordeal of a few hours ago. Although I had been only a few hundred yards away, he hadn't noticed my struggles. I looked at the tender's log. In the past week the bridge had been opened four times. It was a quiet job, he said. I promised him that I'd give him some work later in the morning if the wind abated. Then I walked back

13 Miles

to *Slick Ca'm*.

The Lewes and Rehoboth Canal, the next leg of my journey, is nine miles long. It was opened in 1913 as part of the inland waterway to Chincoteague. The Assawoman Canal, which connects Indian River Bay with Little Assawoman Bay, was already in existence, having been dug in 1890. But neither of these canals was ever busy. The automobile met most of the need. Still, it provided a protected route for small vessels and kept them away from the dreaded cape at Henlopen.

Negotiating the entire 145 miles of the inland waterway from Roosevelt Inlet to Cape Charles had been my initial goal. There are, however, four fixed bridges across Assawoman Canal. I could, of course, lower my mast, which is hinged. But here was a classic example of a double bind: you're damned if you do and damned if you don't. The bridges over the canal have a vertical clearance of four feet. This clearance is measured at mean high water. With the mast down I still needed four and a half feet. A little patience in waiting for a low tide would make this possible. However, water depth is always shown on charts at mean low water; the canal has a controlling depth of only two feet, and I needed two and a half feet underneath me. So, if I waited for the tide to get low enough to get me through the bridges, I would surely run aground. The prospect of being aground underneath a bridge with a rising tide was too painful to contemplate. Therefore, I would have to go outside, at least for a short distance, into the Atlantic Ocean at Indian River, then sail to Ocean City Inlet to bypass Assawoman.

Recently, the U.S. Army Corps of Engineers held hearings on the Delmarva Intercoastal Waterway, as it is now called. The entire length would be dredged to a minimum of a six-foot depth and a width of one hundred feet, and bridges would be removed or replaced by higher ones. All this would cost around fifteen million dollars. There is precious little commercial traffic down the waterway, but the proposed improvement would be a boon to sailors and sport fishermen. The environmental impact has yet to be studied, but the increased traffic is sure to be detrimental to the marshes and wetlands.

By midmorning the wind was down to around fifteen knots. The sun was shining brightly, and it had begun to warm up. I decided to head for Rehoboth Bay. It took me almost as long to get *Slick Ca'm* out of her slip as it had taken to get her in. Part of the problem was the fact that my anchor still sat in the mud in the middle of the channel, 150 feet away. After some struggling I retrieved the anchor and my line. As my engine idled, the current carried me toward the bridge. I blew my horn three times. Nothing happened. Another three blasts. I was now convinced that the tender had fallen asleep, even though I had given him advance warning. I got three answering blasts on the third try. The traffic barrier came down, and the bridge slowly opened—about six feet. I started making a circle and motioned toward the tender to open the bridge higher. He raised it another six feet. Still, it wasn't enough. I kept going in small circles. I may have had delusions of grandeur, but it didn't look to me as if my thirty-foot mast could clear the bridge without going awfully close to the concrete abutment on the right side. The bridge was cocked at an uncomfortably low angle. The operator came out of his office and waved for me to go through. I waved back at him. Did he not understand that I was in a sailboat? With a mast? Back he went into his little cubicle, shaking his head. Another six feet. It looked as if I

could make it now. I headed for the narrow opening. As I got closer, a man jumped out of his waiting car, leaned over the side of the bridge, and shouted, "Go ahead, damn it, you got plenty of room!" I kept on for the bridge, and prayed. I cleared it by an easy ten feet.

Now I was in the canal proper. Never more than a hundred feet wide, it is bordered by marshes and occasional stands of trees, until it emerges into Rehoboth Bay. I hoisted the genoa and turned off and stowed the engine; the wind and the current pushed us along at a respectable four knots. The two remaining drawbridges opened on signal. At one o'clock, near the end of the canal, I turned into the Rehoboth Beach Yacht Basin, where the *Coast Pilot* said I could find water and groceries. Once again, it was wrong. The basin was completely deserted. I dropped the hook, made lunch, and then traversed the few remaining yards to Rehoboth Bay. The channel through the bay was well marked, and with the centerboard up I never touched bottom. One lone fisherman was at work in the wide expanse of the bay.

At three I was in Indian River Bay. Beyond the bridge over Indian River Inlet I could see the angry waves of the ocean lashing across the inlet. The Coast Guard station was still flying the Small Craft Advisory flag. I tied up at a nearby yacht basin and walked over to the Coast Guard to check the weather report for the following day. It looked encouraging. I walked across the bridge and looked down at the ocean and the inlet. The sight was even more terrifying than my first, sea-level look. The tide was rushing out between the narrow breakwater jetties, and the waves, pushed by an onshore wind, broke solidly across the entire width. I did not look forward to going through that. I hoped it would be calmer tomorrow. One week after starting my voyage I would take *Slick Ca'm* out into the ocean.

I went for a long walk along the deserted beach. In another month, thousands of people would be sunbathing. The thought seemed improbable. At six I headed back toward my slip at the basin. After dinner I stood in the companionway and looked toward the Coast Guard building. The red Small Craft Advisory flag was still flying straight out. I crawled into my bunk and read over once more in the *Cruising Guide* the section on negotiating inlets. Somewhat reassured, I fell asleep at sunset.

Indian River Inlet to Ocean City Inlet The cabin temperature was exactly thirty-two degrees when I awoke. My sleeping bag had not been designed for this kind of weather. The sun showed a bright rim just above the dunes. I opened the hatch; it was already warmer outside than it was inside. I dressed, and after breakfast I walked up to the bridge over Indian River Inlet. The scene was placid compared to the previous day. A gentle breeze out of the north barely rippled the water, but there were still huge swells. It looked as if *Slick Ca'm* could handle it, though.

On the way back I stopped to ask the Coast Guard why the red flag was still flying. The duty officer sent a guardsman out to lower it and thanked me for reminding him. The forecast was fine. I went back to *Slick Ca'm* to prepare her for our ocean voyage—all seventeen miles of it. At 8:00 A.M. I motored out of the inlet. It was easier than I had thought, but ago-nizingly slow. We were bucking a flood tide and barely made a knot and a half. But there were no breaking waves, no swirling eddies. Once out beyond the breakwater, I stowed the engine and hoisted sail. A ten-knot breeze was pushing us, and we were occasionally helped by the large swells. I stayed about a quarter mile from the beach, well out of the range of the breaking surf. Except for small stretches of dunes, the coast was heavily built up. Toward noon I could see the Fenwick Island light-house, once in a while obscured by surrounding high-rise buildings. The wind now began shifting toward the southwest and increased to about fifteen knots. Sailing became a bit more exciting now and, rail down, we pushed on toward Ocean City.

For a few months out of the year, Ocean City is the largest city on the Eastern Shore. With a per-manent, year-round population of slightly over 2,000, Ocean City can, and does, accommodate as

The Eighth Day

many as 150,000 visitors on summer weekends. It has been estimated that from 20,000 to 35,000 people can be found per mile of beach, a beach that is getting narrower every year. Ocean-front lots that cost $2,000 per fifty-foot width around the turn of the century now bring $7,000 per *foot*. Although the great building boom did not begin until the 1960s, Ocean City has been around for more than a hundred years.

This lonely, unbroken stretch of sand (Ocean City Inlet did not exist before 1933) stirred the imagination of Isaac Coffin, a farmer who lived on the mainland across Sinepuxent Bay. He envisioned possibilities for a hotel that would accommodate fishermen and perhaps vacationers. In 1867 Coffin decided to investigate the ownership of the beach and soon discovered that it belonged to Stephen Tabor, a New York resident. A land grant from Lord Baltimore in the 1700s had put the property into the hands of Tabor's family.

Coffin's inquiries made Tabor uneasy, and he asked the Maryland legislature to confirm his patent, which it did. But Tabor lived too far away to "develop" his beach properly and so he offered, instead, to give a plot of land to anyone who would build a hotel on it. This was, of course, exactly what Coffin had had in mind. In 1869 he built a tiny hotel and tavern on his newly acquired property and called it the Rhode Island Inn. Legend has it that he found a ship's nameboard washed up on the beach and nailed it up, thereby naming his inn. The hotel was a success, and other businessmen and investors became interested. The Synepuxent Beach Corporation was formed and, in 1875, built a 210-room hotel, the Atlantic, for $75,000. Ocean City was on the map. Transportation, however, still left something to be desired. The only way to get there was by boat

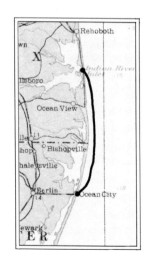

across Sinepuxent Bay, after a difficult journey from Baltimore.

One of the founding members of the Synepuxent Beach Corporation, Colonel Lemuel Showell, owned a railroad. He had it built to haul farm produce and lumber between Berlin and Salisbury, a distance of twenty-two miles. Ocean City is only seven miles from Berlin, and in 1876, with Ocean City enjoying its first boom, the Colonel built an extension to the edge of Sinepuxent Bay. Baltimoreans would travel via Wilmington and then transfer to the Wicomico and Pocomoke Railroad. But they still had to be rowed. The railroad was so successful, however, that a bridge to Ocean City was built a few years later. The resort was heavily advertised. One brochure, after expounding all the marvels of the journey and the excellence of the hotels, said: "Among the attractions of Ocean City we must not forget to mention the ocean."

In 1891 the Baltimore and Eastern Shore Railway was built. It ran from Claiborne, where the ferries from the western shore docked, to Salisbury, where it connected with Showell's line. The eighty-six-mile journey took only a little over two hours, a respectable time even today by automobile. Soon Ocean City boasted a dozen hotels and numerous cottages for paying guests. The boardwalk at first was a temporary affair, laid down the first week of July and taken up in the middle of September. Finally, in 1916, the first vehicular bridge across Sinepuxent Bay was built to handle the increasing automobile traffic.

On August 23, 1933, a freak summer storm cut an inlet across the beach just south of the town. Ocean City now had access to the Atlantic Ocean and a safe harbor behind the beach—if the inlet could be held open. Just as the sea had cut the inlet so it could close it again, as had happened several times on that coast. The Army Corps of Engineers built jetties and revetments to help keep the inlet open. Within a few years, Ocean City's Chamber of Commerce would proudly call it the Marlin Capital of the World.

But in early May the beaches were still deserted. By midafternoon I sailed through Ocean City Inlet, and my minor ocean voyage was over. It had been an uneventful, even boring, sail. I would much rather sail through canals, marshes, and creeks, where the scenery is constantly changing. And the miles-long stretches of high-rise buildings seemed oddly out of place on the otherwise low and tranquil Eastern Shore. I anchored near the deep-sea fishing boats and made an early dinner. I went to sleep at dusk, anxious to begin my voyage behind the barrier islands—the loneliest part of the journey.

Ocean City Inlet to Greenbackville Harbor It was a beautiful morning. The wind, still out of the southwest, kept me from sailing through the narrow channel past Assateague Island until I reached the wider waters of Chincoteague Bay. But it would be warm; already at sunrise the temperature was in the upper forties. As I motored into the channel and looked back, I was struck by the contrast between Ocean City behind me, looking like Lower Manhattan, and Assateague Island ahead, deserted and barren on the other side of the inlet.

The Eastern Shore from here south to Cape Charles is bordered, and for the most part protected, by a string of barrier islands and shallow bays, marshes, and mud flats that separate it from the mainland. Assateague is the first of those barrier islands. All the islands—Assateague, Wallops, Assawoman, Metomkin, Cedar, Parramore, Hog, Cobb, Wreck, Ship Shoal, Myrtle, and Smith—are uninhabited, except for an occasional cottage on Assateague, the NASA installation on Wallops, and a Coast Guard station on Parramore Island. The waters behind these islands are little used, except by local fishermen. There are a number of navigable inlets between the islands, but the frequently shifting sandbars make their passage difficult, except with local knowledge. The dearth of safe and deep inlets and the abundance of shoals make mariners dread this portion of the coast. Most yachtsmen prefer the route through the Chesapeake, which, although longer, is protected.

As soon as I was in the narrow channel of Sinepuxent Bay, no more than a half mile from Ocean City, I saw a small herd of the famous Chincoteague ponies grazing near the water's edge. The channel, about sixty feet wide, is marked clearly by numbered posts and buoys at

The Ninth Day

regular intervals. Going south, it was even numbers to the right, odd numbers to the left. As long as I headed in a straight line from one to the next, I would presumably have at least three or four feet of water under me.

Two hundred years ago Assateague Island was divided in two by Sinepuxent Inlet, which has since completely disappeared. This inlet was used to smuggle supplies into Maryland during the Revolutionary War, when the Chesapeake was blockaded at its mouth.

Here, too, was the first known landing on the Eastern Shore by Europeans. In the spring of 1524, Giovanni da Verrazano, a Florentine in the employ of King Francis I of France, sailed his *Dauphine* along the Eastern Shore. Other explorers had probably seen the Shore, but Verrazano actually entered Chincoteague Bay and with a number of men from his ship walked nearly eight miles to the headwaters of the Pocomoke River. He called the country Arcadia, a lovely name that has not survived.

When Verrazano stepped ashore, he saw a naked Indian youth, apparently a member of the Assateague tribe. The youth, obviously frightened, made some friendly gestures. One of Verrazano's sailors, perhaps misinterpreting the gesture, fired his musket into the air. The young warrior, according to Verrazano's account, "prayed, worshipping like a monk, lifting his finger towards the sky and pointing to the ship and the sea, he appeared to bless us." When the landing party tried to approach him more closely, he fled into the forest.

Verrazano saw other Indians when he came near the swamps of the Pocomoke River, but they all fled in terror. The explorers tried to capture two women, an old woman and a young girl "of much beauty and tall of stature," but the women's

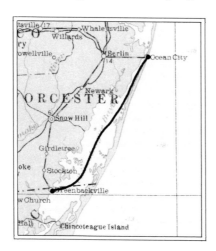

screams apparently intimidated them. Verrazano and his men went back to their ship and sailed on. It would be nearly a hundred years before the Indians would see a European again.

At noon I entered Chincoteague Bay. Although the bay is very shallow—I couldn't find one spot on the chart where the depth exceeded seven feet—at least I could sail here. The sky had become overcast, and the rain, due for some time now, seemed to be on its way. The wind increased to about twenty knots, and a mean chop began kicking up. I shut off the engine and stowed it, then raised the main and the working jib and began the long beat toward Greenbackville. I had no special reason for going there, but I was intrigued by the name. The town is located just inside the Virginia border on the mainland. This would be the third state I visited.

At one o'clock it began to rain hard. Visibility was bad, and I was glad I had laid compass courses earlier in the day. The buoys were hard to locate, for some were two and three miles apart. I was busy dodging crab pots, seine nets, and shoals, but even in the rain the sailing was some of the best I had done so far. At three I was near Greenbackville and realized that the glorious wet sailing had made me forget all about lunch. I ducked into the dilapidated harbor. Greenbackville had seen its best years long ago. Wrecks were strewn all over the edge of the tiny harbor. I tied up to the remains of what once must have been a public landing. This was a ghost town. No one was in sight. After lunch I walked around the little village. I couldn't find a store anywhere. The place gave me the creeps.

A thunderstorm came through around five. It didn't amount to much. I went down into the cabin, closed the hatch and curtains, and took a nap.

Then someone stepped on deck. The slight motion of the boat and the sound woke me instantly. A boy, about ten years old, was trying to peer down into the cabin through the companionway. He was as startled as I was. "I'm sorry. I didn't mean to," he said, and scrambled back onto the dock. I stuck my head out of the hatch. "Come on," I said. "It's okay to look around if you want to." He shyly stepped back on board. He was just down checking his crab float, he said, and "there weren't never no yachts that came into Greenbackville." I showed him around *Slick Ca'm*'s tiny cabin, all of which could be seen without going down below. He was obviously impressed by the compact arrangement and likened it to a camping trailer.

After a while I became used to his accent, and we talked about fishing, school, and sailing, which he had never done. He asked if a little boat like mine could sail to England. I said she could, although I wasn't sure I was the one to take her there. The remainder of the conversation revolved around how many Coca-Colas it would take to sustain him on just such a voyage. My young visitor left to go home for supper, the first intimation I had that there were other people living in Greenbackville.

The rain has stopped. While I made dinner in the hour before dark, I entertained two more visitors, both older men. As if rehearsed, the first comment in each case was, "Nice rig you got there." Then I heard about how Greenbackville got its name (the oyster business at the end of the last century made nearly everyone rich) and about the good old days. They both agreed that this was a dead town. And as each visitor left, small talk exhausted, their parting comment was "You can't even get a loaf of bread in this place any more." I knew that. I'd tried it. At sunset I was alone again and soon turned in for the night.

Greenbackville Harbor to Chincoteague Channel
It was a bright and beautiful morning. Greenbackville harbor was quiet. I noticed that some of
the crabbing boats were missing, but I had not
heard them leave. I had overslept, and the sun
was already high. It was nearly eight o'clock. It
occurred to me that my long sleep had something
to do with the fact that on this day I would only
sail a few miles. Chincoteague, a mere seven miles
across the bay, was the next stop. Although not
quite the halfway point in my journey, it marked
the beginning of the stretch I most looked forward to (and was most apprehensive about).
Chincoteague would be the last port in which to
find supplies, at least for a while. The comments
of some of the citizens of Greenbackville still
stuck in my mind; if they couldn't even buy a loaf
of bread here, suppose I got stuck on a mud flat in
the marshes somewhere. I still wasn't really sure
that anybody actually lived in Greenbackville.
Here I was, tied up at the town landing (at least
the remains of it) on a glorious day, and all during
breakfast and my unhurried preparations for departure I never saw a soul, or even a car. As I prepared to cast off a cat slunk by and hissed at me.

In a warm, steady breeze I sailed out of Greenbackville at nine on the dot. I could see some of
the crabbers, scattered around the horizon, working their pots. Rather than head directly for
Chincoteague, I decided to dawdle the morning
away sailing Chincoteague Bay in this wonderful
breeze. My desire to sail aimlessly awhile was
aided immeasurably by the fact that I could for
the first time sail without my foul-weather clothes.
It was actually warm. I would sail, lee gunwales
buried in the water, until the board scraped the
bottom near the shore, and then I would tack,
head toward the opposite shore, and repeat the

The Tenth Day

procedure. I even sailed back across the Maryland-Virginia line just north of Greenbackville.

At noon I headed for the narrow channel that leads toward the town of Chincoteague. Reluctantly I lowered and furled the sails and started the engine. Sailing a mile through the sixty-foot-wide channel would be a real chore, for the wind was straight out of the south now. As I motored through the channel, whose eastern edge borders the backyards of many of the houses of Chincoteague, a man on crutches hobbled toward the water's edge. He was dressed in a Coast Guard uniform, with petty officer's insignia. I raised my hand in greeting and throttled down. "Where you headed?" he shouted. I told him I was headed for the Coast Guard base. "I don't think you can clear the bridge!" he said solicitously. I knew I couldn't clear the bridge. With its fifteen feet of clearance I'd have exactly half my mast left. The bridge would have to open. "I'll blow my horn to warn the tender," I said. He nodded with what I thought looked like sympathy. Then, as fast as he could on his crutches, he made his way toward his car.

When I got to within a few hundred yards of the bascule bridge that connects Chincoteague with the mainland, I blew my horn three times. Nothing happened. But it was warm, I wasn't in a hurry, and besides, I was in the South now. I'd have to adjust. I began making great circles in front of the bridge. Still no answering blast. After a few more minutes had elapsed, I saw a car, the car that belonged to the man on crutches, speed across the bridge and stop at the bridge tender's control house. A figure leaped out of the passenger side. The bridge tender had arrived on duty. He dashed up the steps to his office, gave three shattering blasts on his horn, and lowered the traffic barriers. Slowly the bridge tilted up. I went

through, waved, and headed for the Coast Guard station just beyond the bridge. The man on crutches was standing at the end of the pier. I threw him my bowline, and he expertly tied me to one of the pilings. I shut off the engine.

"I went in my car to get the bridge tender," he said. "I figured he wasn't where he was supposed to be, though you'd think he'd be more attentive to his job. Last year, when there was an opening, more than 175 people applied for the $2.75-an-hour job. But it's boring work. Sailboats are rare. I'm about the only sailor in town." He sat down on one of the pilings and continued: "I was watching you through my glasses when you took your sails down. I figured you were headed for the bridge. You were smart not to try and sail the channel." I had found a fellow sailor, and we talked sailing. I offered to take him out for a sail, but his recent foot operation prevented him from accepting my invitation. "Come back," he said, "when I'm off these crutches. Perhaps the breeze will be just as it was this morning." He limped off.

After lunch I spent an enlightening hour with Jerry Shelton, the officer in charge of the Coast Guard buoy tender that services aids to navigation from Chincoteague down to Cape Charles. Few men know the marshes, channels, and inlets as well as he does. We went over the charts inch by inch, with Jerry pointing out the most recent changes in the constantly shifting channels. "You won't have any trouble," he assured me. "And you'll have a great time. My boat draws four feet, and although we sometimes have to plow our way out of the sand and mud, it's mostly no trouble at all." He pointed out interesting islands and channels. I thought I detected a hint of envy on his part, and I asked him if my hunch was right. "Sure," he said, "especially if you're not on duty, and you could take your time. There's a lot of pretty scenery along the way. But when we're out there, we have a job to do, and we do it as fast and as well as we can."

I was allowed to remain tied up to the dock until evening. I walked into town to do my shopping and stopped on the way, on a sudden impulse, at the library. I asked the librarian about *Misty of Chincoteague*, the phenomenally successful children's book by Marguerite Henry, inspired by the legends of the Chincoteague ponies. The librarian had several copies. "But the children in town don't borrow it," she said. "They've all read it. It's the kids here on summer holidays who check it out when it rains."

The legends, actively promoted by the Chincoteague Chamber of Commerce, say that these Chincoteague ponies (neither ponies nor living on Chincoteague) are the descendants of horses carried aboard a Spanish galleon that was shipwrecked on this coast. Other stories insist that pirates allowed their horses to graze on the island. The ponies are actually the descendants of European horses brought to the Eastern Shore in the seventeenth century. The animals live on Assateague Island, and the herd is kept down to about two hundred animals, the number which the island can comfortably support.

The barrier islands were recognized as excellent grazing grounds for horses and cattle, and they had the added advantage of not having to be fenced. But many horses escaped, or swam to the mainland, and in 1671 it was reported that large numbers were roaming freely in Somerset and Accomack counties. Destruction of crops by the wild animals was so great that for a time the importation of horses was forbidden. Young gentlemen on the lower Eastern Shore hunted the

horses with dogs. Over the years a unique breed of stunted horses developed, actually somewhat larger than a pony. Today the only herd remains on Assateague, where the animals live year round, feeding on marsh grass and myrtle leaves.

By 1845 the Assateague herd had been considerably reduced in number, for the healthiest and strongest ponies had been culled out for use or sale by the islanders. "Pony penning," which started in the early 1800s, is now done annually, under the supervision, and for the benefit, of the Chincoteague Volunteer Fire Department. Toward the end of July, the ponies are rounded up and forced to swim across Assateague Channel to Chincoteague, where part of the herd is sold at auction, after which the remaining ponies are allowed to swim back across the channel for another year of freedom on the thirty-three-mile-long island. In 1974 fifty ponies were sold for an average of a hundred dollars each (compared to ten dollars fifty years ago) while forty thousand people watched.

As I walked farther into the town, I remembered an article in *Scribner's* magazine of nearly a hundred years ago, which I had read before setting out on my voyage. It described Chincoteague this way: "This island is inhabited by oystermen and wreckers, inoffensive heathens in mode and talk." But that was before tourism was discovered by Chincoteague; tourism is now the island's biggest business. And the biggest attraction is the Assateague Island National Seashore, the only accessible unspoiled beach between Cape Cod and Cape Hatteras.

As early as 1935 the federal government explored the possibilities of protecting Assateague Island from commercial and residential development. More than 93 percent of the Atlantic Ocean shore between New York and Virginia is privately owned, and Assateague was one of the last remaining virgin stretches of beach. In 1943 one-third of the island was declared the Chincoteague

National Wildlife Refuge. It is a mecca for bird watchers; ninety-two species of birds breed on the island and more than three hundred species have been observed.

The State of Maryland acquired 680 acres as a park in the northern portion, and in 1965 federal legislation created the National Seashore. A toll bridge had been built in 1962 from Chincoteague to Assateague, so that the island could be easily reached.

Another attraction of Chincoteague, now in name only, is the famous Chincoteague oyster, many of which came from Toms Cove, a fine harbor of refuge on the lower end of the island. Toms Cove eventually shoaled severely and became one of the nation's most coveted oyster grounds. Toms Cove oysters, often ordered by name, were a prized delicacy for a century. But a mysterious disease (MSX—mononucleate sphere unknown) began plaguing the oyster culture in the early 1960s, and growing oysters is now a minor industry on the island. Many Chesapeake Bay oysters are transplanted to the saltier waters around Chincoteague for a day or so and then shipped and sold as "Chincoteague oysters."

After my grocery-buying spree I carried my bags back to *Slick Ca'm*. I stowed my supplies and, casting off my lines, moved to an anchorage on the other side of Chincoteague Channel. I spent the rest of the day reading about the part of the world I was about to enter and studying the relevant charts. The V.I.P., Jerry Shelton had called it—the Virginia Inside Passage. The route is used almost exclusively by local watermen, although a few sport-fishing enthusiasts use the dredged channels on weekends to reach the ocean through some of the inlets. I made an early dinner, then watched the sun set across the marshes, and went to sleep.

Chincoteague Channel to Folly Creek The sport fishermen were out already when I awoke at sunrise. It was Saturday, and Chincoteague Channel near the inlet was already crowded with dozens of motorboats and hopeful fishermen. A fresh and steady breeze was blowing out of the north. With main and genoa hoisted, I dodged the fleet. Judging by the comments and expressions of the anglers, a sailboat in this part of the world was a rare sight. After I passed Chincoteague Inlet (a redundancy—Chincoteague means "inlet") the channel became considerably narrower, and I sailed behind Wallops Island, through Island Hole Narrows, Ballast Narrows, and Cat Creek, each with increasingly sharp turns. Sometimes the twisting channels would double back on themselves, and I would be tacking or reaching instead of running. The marshes, dotted with herons, spread out for miles on both sides of the channel. Occasionally I hesitated, for new channels would appear and confuse me, but between the charts and the Coast Guard's daymarks I made few errors in navigation. Once in a while the board touched bottom when I tacked too close to the edge of the channel, but the soft mud quickly released its hold when I raised the board.

Now there was not a boat in sight—just miles of marsh grass ahead, the dark water below, and hazy skies overhead. This was the most demanding sailing I had done so far and also the most enjoyable. The steady breeze swept unhindered across the marshes, yet the narrow waterways, protected by the marsh grass on all sides, never even got ruffled. Just before I entered Northam Narrows, a fisherman passed me in a small outboard. "I hope you have a centerboard," he shouted. But with the high tide, draft was not yet a problem.

The Eleventh Day

After passing behind Assawoman Island and through Kegotank Bay, I was closer to the ocean. I could hear the surf breaking a hundred yards beyond the low dunes. I sailed *Slick Ca'm* close to the edge of the channel and discovered that the water was deep enough near the island to enable me to sail right up to the shore. I headed into the wind and jumped onto the island with anchor in hand. I dug the Danforth deep into the soil, then jumped back aboard and lowered the sails. With *Slick Ca'm* safely tethered, I explored the narrow strip of sand that separated the V.I.P. and the Atlantic Ocean. Assawoman Island is just a few feet higher than the waters surrounding it. It was easy to imagine new inlets being cut through in a storm. I walked on the beach for an hour, all the while keeping a weather eye on *Slick Ca'm*, and collected conch shells. But there were so many strewn on the beach, each more perfect than the

next, that I soon had to give up; room aboard *Slick Ca'm* was limited. I kept the three smallest. As I approached my boat again after my long walk, I was struck by the contrast in the scene I surveyed—*Slick Ca'm* riding serenely in the channel in front of me and behind me the crashing surf of the ocean. I stepped back aboard my sloop, dislodged the anchor, and continued my meandering, twisting progress.

The next island was Metomkin. The channel behind it is called Wire Passage. On the chart it looks a little like wire—barbed wire. Tiny guts and streams shoot off from the main channel in clusters. As I silently passed a small fishing skiff, an old waterman in the boat called out, "Where you headed?" "Cape Charles," I replied. "I envy you. I envy you!" he answered, smiling.

I crossed Metomkin Bay at five. The haze had turned to a dense fog. Visibility was less than an

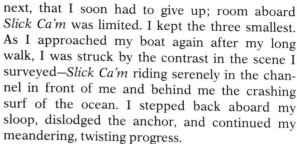

21 Miles

eighth of a mile, and between markers 84 and 85 I ran hard aground. It was low tide. I sheeted in the sails and tried to make *Slick Ca'm* heel over as much as possible; she would not draw as much water that way. But it didn't work. The channel was about thirty feet wide, according to the chart, but the dark water would not yield the secret of its exact location. Metomkin Bay is nearly two miles wide, and there were no landmarks I could take bearings on. In clear weather it might have been a cinch, but I was halfway between two markers, and I couldn't see either one. I was going to have to kedge off. I intended to walk the anchor out a way, then try to winch off the shoal back into the channel, once I found the channel. It wasn't necessary. A small outboard-powered skiff appeared out of the fog. Its captain quietly hailed me: "You missed the channel by about six feet. Not bad in this kind of weather. Throw me your line." I wondered how he knew I was six feet out of the channel. I threw him my line. Without another word he gently pulled me off the mudbank and back into the channel. I waved my thanks. He waved back and disappeared into the fog again.

At marker 86 navigating became easy again, even in the fog. The bay narrowed into a tiny gut, and the nearby marshes made the course easily identifiable. At marker 87, instead of continuing in the waterway, I turned west into Folly Creek. (In the 1600s "folly" meant a clump of trees as well as foolishness.) Clearly it would be folly to go on. It was almost dark now, and rain and thirty-knot winds were in the forecast. Folly Creek was as snug an anchorage as I would be able to find in this flat, open country. After I anchored near the head of the creek the fog closed in even further. I wondered whether, if the fog never lifted, I would be able to find my way out of the maze of guts, channels, and marshes. But I was in a place of peace and simplicity. The pleasure of having been able to sail the Inside Passage, the multitude of birds, and the serenity of the landscape made me wish that Verrazano could have made the name Arcadia stick.

Folly Creek to Horseshoe Lead Night changed imperceptibly into day. The hazy outlines simply became lighter, not clearer. I could see only the edge of the creek. Whatever was beyond was hidden in a dense, low cloud. After breakfast I decided to inch my way back toward the V.I.P., and if I couldn't find the markers at all, I would just anchor and wait until the fog cleared. I needed the compass to tell me which direction to head out in. Both sides of the creek looked identical. I headed east under power, but ever so slowly.

Once I was out of Folly and into Longboat Creek the fog lifted in a sudden gust of wind. The landscape revealed itself in seconds: the monotony of the marshes ahead, the delicate traceries of the trees on the mainland to my right, the low sandy outline of Cedar Island to the east. It was impossible to sail, though. The wind was dead ahead, and there was no room to tack in the narrow cuts. It was only ten miles to Wachapreague, across Burtons Bay, but getting there took three hours of plowing into the white-capped waves.

Wachapreague ("little city by the sea"), as the Machinpungo Indians called it, was once a thriving port, where many coastal schooners called. There even was a New York–Wachapreague freight line at the turn of the century. As the seafood business declined, and trains and trucks took over the transportation needs, the sport-fishing industry in Wachapreague grew. Now the town, with a population of a little over four hundred, is dominated by Hotel Wachapreague, built in 1902, a favorite of the fishermen who invade the town on weekends.

The Eastern Shore peninsula here is very narrow; the Chesapeake is less than ten miles away. Yet clear distinctions are made between the "baysiders," on the Chesapeake side, and the "seasiders," on the ocean side. Those born and raised somewhere in between are referred to as "highlanders." The highest land on this part of the Eastern Shore is perhaps twenty feet above sea level.

The two Virginia counties that constitute part of the lower Eastern Shore, Accomack and Northampton, were among the first to be settled in Virginia. The Eastern Shore Indians, of Algonquin stock, owed allegiance to Powhatan (of John Smith and Pocahontas fame) in a loose confederation during the early seventeenth century. This part of the Eastern Shore was called Accowmack by Indian tribes on the other side of the Chesapeake. The word conveyed the sense of isolation and remoteness; it means "the place on the other side of the water." When the first census was taken on the Eastern Shore, in 1634, a quarter century after Jamestown was first settled, the European population numbered only seventy-six, but already some of the In-

dians were being forced farther north.

I motored into Wachapreague and tied up to one of the docks. The little town was quiet. I walked through it for a while, admiring the gingerbread on some of the houses, then sauntered back toward the docks, bought some ice, and fell to talking with a recent, part-time resident of Wachapreague. My informant, a tall, bearded, bespectacled man in his late thirties, was a professor of mechanical engineering at New York University. He had discovered Wachapreague a year earlier, and since then he had bought a house, restored it, and spent every weekend, summer and winter, in the little town. The six-hour drives on Friday and Sunday nights were easily worth it, he said. He talked about the townspeople, the long growing season and the subdued beauty of the landscape, and he rhapsodized about the beaches of the barrier islands. His enthusiasm

was infectious. Remembering my brief sojourn on Assawoman Island, I decided to investigate the island he loved best, Parramore.

I cast off and motored the few miles through the marshes to the island. The wind was now gusting to thirty miles, and the trip turned out to be agonizingly long. Bucking both the wind and the tide, we took more than an hour to cover the two and a half miles. At one of the sharp turns in the channel my centerboard loudly scraped the bottom. I pulled on the rope to raise the board and fell back into the cockpit holding the rope in my hand. The rope had chafed through, probably worn by all the groundings I had experienced. I was now drawing five feet whether I liked it or not.

I had intended to anchor off Parramore and wade to shore, but now I decided to make for the Coast Guard station on the island. Perhaps they would be able to help me locate a boatyard where I could haul *Slick Ca'm* and splice a new line to her board. As I neared the station, four guardsmen, who had been watching my slow progress, ran out to help me with my lines. This isolated station does not get many visitors, and its occupants were glad to be of help. The officer in charge made some phone calls to Wachapreague, Willis Wharf, Quinby, and Oyster, but not one yard could haul me for at least three days. I asked about the possibility of engaging a scuba diver. The obliging officer dialed another number, chatted for a few minutes, then hung up. "He'll meet you in Wachapreague tomorrow morning," he said. I asked if I could stay tied to his pier and walk around the island, and was given permission. The weather looked even more threatening. I double-checked my lines, then headed for Parramore's ocean beach.

Seven miles long, and over a mile wide, the island is for the most part densely wooded, with hundreds of deer roaming freely. I walked the shore bordering Wachapreague Inlet, then turned south on the wide, wind-swept beach. The wind seemed even stronger here, and sand blasted my face during each gust. After I had walked a mile along the edge of the ocean it started to rain. I turned inland and walked behind the dunes back toward the Coast Guard dock, where I was told I would have to move my boat. Severe storm warnings had been issued while I was walking the beach, and staying tied up to the dock was not the smartest move. I agreed; in a blow, being tethered to a dock is foolish. The proper place for *Slick Ca'm* would be riding free, at anchor, where there would be least resistance. I crawled into my foul-weather gear again, pulled on my boots, started the engine, and headed down Horseshoe Lead for about a mile. Here I was somewhat protected, for the wind was still blowing out of the southeast. But the storm would probably come out of the northwest. In addition, a tornado watch was on,

and large hailstones were presumably also in the offing. The warning would be in effect until ten; it was now six o'clock.

I carefully set the anchor in twenty feet of water, let out all 150 feet of my anchor line, and wrapped chafe guards around the area where the line rubbed the chocks. The sky looked ominous. I made dinner and finished cleaning up just before the wind shifted and the squalls came through. Violent rain and hail pelted *Slick Ca'm*. The storm raged and rattled for two hours. The wind, sometimes up to forty-five knots (according to the Coast Guard), whipped the waters around us into a froth. But the anchor held, and at nine o'clock the worst was over. I had been awed by the spectacle and had gained new confidence in my boat and her gear. I poured myself a glass of whiskey, to celebrate our emerging unscathed, and resolved to get up early to have my centerboard fixed in Wachapreague. I was asleep ten minutes later.

Horseshoe Lead to Oyster Harbor The morning brought clear skies and a brisk northwesterly breeze, perfect for the next leg of the Virginia Inside Passage. But first the centerboard had to be repaired. By seven I was under way. I had considerable difficulty in extricating the anchor from the bottom; it had really dug in during the blow, but this was a small price to pay for the security it had given. I motored the few miles back to Wachapreague. At the end of one of the piers a man I judged to be in his seventies stood watching me. "You can tie up here," he said, and without another word turned around and walked back to a shed on the other side of the pier. I tied up and followed him. I asked if this was the place where the scuba diver was going to meet me. He seemed annoyed by my question, but I didn't think he was the diver. "He'll be here by and by," he said as he continued to plane a board on his workbench. It was obviously all the information he was going to give me.

"By and by" turned out to take exactly two hours and twenty minutes. I didn't want to act like one of those Yankees who always seem to be in a hurry, so I kept a low profile; I aired the sleeping bag, cleaned the cabin, then took a nap in the cockpit. Finally, at ten-thirty, the old man appeared on the pier again, followed by a man with a crew cut, in his early thirties, carrying air tanks and a tool kit. I thought this might be a good time to ask what all this was going to cost me. "Thirty dollars," the older man said, spitting some tobacco into the harbor. Thinking that that might be an hourly fee, and not knowing how many hours might be involved, I exclaimed, "Wow!" It was a mistake. Without a word the older man picked up the diver's tanks and walked off the pier. The diver, already stripped to his bathing trunks, fol-

The Thirteenth Day

lowed. I jumped up on the pier and followed them. The old man was muttering something about "all you people" being the same. He then stopped, turned around to face me, and said, "You can go somewhere else and get the damn thing fixed." The diver remained quiet. Apparently he was the subcontractor. I explained that my "Wow" was in no way to be construed as a comment on his pricing practices. It then became clear that thirty dollars was what I would be charged regardless of the length of time the job might take. Now it seemed a bargain. Still, only after fifteen minutes of small talk and apologies did the old man reluctantly consent. "Go ahead, Dave, if you want. And if he can't pay for it, I will." I helped carry the diving gear back to *Slick Ca'm*. Dave strapped on his air tanks and disappeared below the water. In half an hour a new line had been spliced and the centerboard was working

again. I gladly paid the thirty dollars and soon was on my way, with main and genoa wing and wing, before the spanking breeze.

The marshes alternated with wide, shallow bays. The desire to cut the navigation markers too close was sometimes overwhelming. Often there was water as far as I could see. Yet when I deviated from the channel by only a few feet, my board would again start scraping the bottom. I sailed past Parramore, Hog, and then Cobb islands, which are the most beautiful of the barrier islands.

All the islands were inhabited two hundred years ago, mostly by fishermen. Parramore, named after a Thomas Parramore who owned the island in the seventeenth century, was shown on maps published after 1700 as Teach's Island. This led to the assumption that the dreaded Edward Teach—Blackbeard— had made the island one of his haunts. But a map made by Augustine Herman in 1673, before Black-

beard's days, shows Fetches Island, so it seems reasonable to assume that Teach's is a corruption of Fetches. But legends about Blackbeard persist, even though it is known that he never sailed north of the Chesapeake capes.

Until 1948 there was a lighthouse on Hog Island. The island had seen many shipwrecks, for its shoals extend far into the ocean. One of the worst disasters occurred on December 27, 1797, when the HMS *Hunter* was wrecked on Hog Island; seventy-five sailors out of a crew of eighty perished. The first Hog Island lighthouse was built in 1854. This was a stone structure that was replaced in 1896 by a new, higher, skeleton tower, some three thousand feet north of the original beacon.

On February 22, 1900, the lighthouse was attacked by an enormous flock of birds. Several hours after sunset, attracted by the intense light, thousands of birds (species not recorded) began pecking at the glass panes of the lantern. The keeper on duty summoned his assistants, and for the next hour and a half they fired at the birds with double-barreled shotguns. Sixty-eight birds were killed that night. Several days later the birds attacked again. Having used all their ammunition during the first assault, the keepers resorted to clubs, killing nearly 150 birds. Nevertheless, the birds succeeded in breaking several panes and extinguishing the light. The incident was never repeated. The lighthouse, severely undermined by the encroaching sea, was torn down in 1948.

After the memorable winter storm of 1933 the Hog Island residents finally gave up trying to fight the elements. Many of their houses were destroyed in the storm, and the few remaining structures were loaded on barges and floated to safer places on the mainland.

Little is known about the inhabitants of the barrier islands during the eighteenth century, but we do know that the islands were frequented, if not settled. A handwritten notice, dated March 14, 1764, and signed by the collector of customs at Accomac, survives, warning that "Notice is hereby given that all persons who were concern'd in Secreting any part of the Whale, or anthing thereto belonging, on Hog Island or the Island adjacent, will be prosecuted with the utmost Rigour of the Law, and all persons are forbid at their Peril purchasing any part thereof...."

Cobb Island, the next in the chain, was a resort island in the latter half of the nineteenth century. It was welcoming guests at least as early as 1867, for an advertisement in the Baltimore *Sun*, on June 9, 1868, refers to the previous year's success. After praising the bowling alley and billiard room at the hotel, the advertisement continues: "a band of music has been arranged for.... The table arrangements, which gave general satisfaction last year, will be further improved, having engaged the best cook in Virginia, with first class, attentive service.... No accident from surf bathing has ever taken place at this beautiful beach. The shooting and fishing advantages are unequalled on this continent. Terms $3 a day; $18 a week; $60 a month." The hotel, which closed in 1890, drew vacationers and hunters mostly from Baltimore, Washington, and Richmond. The island was also a favorite for plume-hunters, egg collectors, and market gunners. The millinery trade paid excellent prices for tern feathers, and in 1902 one of the owners of Cobb Island proudly reported that he and a helper had killed a record 2,800 terns in three days. The birds were sold in New York for ten cents each. Eventually the Audubon Society was instrumental in protecting the birds on these islands.

After I sailed past Cobb Island, I turned due west

into Sand Shoal Channel and headed for the little town of Oyster. The breeze held beautifully, but it was beginning to get dark. I negotiated the narrow entrance, still under sail, and entered the tiny harbor. Several large fishing boats were tied to the wharves, unloading huge, fist-sized sea clams. I sailed close alongside one of the vessels and asked the captain if they were edible. "Howard Johnson thinks so," he replied. "Come on alongside and I'll give you some." I headed into the wind, lowered sails, and under power turned back toward the fishing boat. The captain lowered a bucket of clams, then came aboard to show me how to clean them and to suggest several ways of cooking them.

The sun had set. I thanked the provider for my fresh seafood dinner, then anchored in the middle of the harbor. I cleaned and sautéed a few of the clams. They were delicious, but three was all I could consume. I threw the others back in the harbor and wondered if they would survive. The noisy process of unloading the fishing boats went on nearly all night, but I was too tired to care after my long, exhilarating sail. Tomorrow I would round Cape Charles and begin the meandering journey back up the Chesapeake Bay.

Oyster Harbor to Kings Creek Most of the fishing boats in the harbor were gone by the time I got up. So were my hopes of setting out under sail. During the night the wind had shifted to the south, and there would be no way I could tack in the few remaining narrow channels. The alternative was to wait. But with nearly two weeks of my time gone, and the myriads of rivers and creeks on the Chesapeake still ahead of me, I decided to proceed under power.

I headed for marker 233, the first outside of Oyster; when I reached marker 268, the last one on the Virginia Inside Passage, I would be in the Chesapeake again. The two-hour trip was uneventful, with the outboard motor quietly purring in its well. Through the Thoroughfare we went, then down Magothy Bay, to the entrance of Smith Island Bay. With the lighthouse on Smith Island (not to be confused with Smith Island in the Chesapeake, north of Tangier Island) in view, I turned at marker 262 and headed southeast for the dredged cut through Cape Charles.

Smith Island (the lower portion came to be called Myrtle, after a storm cut Smith Island in half in 1851) was the site of the first industry on the Eastern Shore. In 1613 Captain Samuel Argoll, after he sailed in his shallop "to discover the east side of the bay," reported: "We also discovered a multitude of Islands bearing good meadow ground, and as I think, Salt might easily be made there, if there were any ponds digged, for that I found Salt Kerned where the water had over-flowne in certain places. Here also is a great store of fish, both Shel-Fish and other."

The following year Sir Thomas Dale, then acting governor of Virginia, sent a party from Jamestown to catch fish and make salt on Smith Island, but in 1617 the salt works were described as "wholly gone to rack and lett fall," even though the Jamestown colonists were "exceedingly distempered by eating pork and other meats fresh and unseasoned."

In 1692 there were reports that pirates were operating around the Capes, and a lookout was established on Smith Island. The orders read "to Range and Scout att least once a weeke upon Smiths Island, where it is most open to the Maine Ocean and the Entringe within the Capes and everyday else to look out on the Bay Side." No pirates were ever discovered, either on the ocean or the bay side of the Eastern Shore.

At noon I motored around the tip of the peninsula, crossed underneath the eastern span of the Chesapeake Bay Bridge Tunnel, passed the last marker, 268, and was back in the Chesapeake again after ten days. Having changed directions, and no longer having to contend with narrow channels, I hoisted sail in the wider waters of the Chesapeake.

The Chesapeake Bay Bridge and Tunnel, completed in 1964, took three and a half years to build. At 17.6 miles it is the longest bridge-tunnel in the world and one of the costliest—$200 million. Seven ferries had previously provided the link from the lower Eastern Shore to the Norfolk–Hampton Roads area. The ferry ride took an hour and a half. The new link gets an automobile across the bay in less than thirty minutes. The first idea had been to build a huge bridge all the way across, but the U.S. Navy objected. The thought that ruins of a bombed bridge might prevent the fleet in Norfolk from reaching the ocean caused nightmares. And so a system of bridges and tunnels was designed— twelve miles of bridges, built on hundreds of concrete trestle legs, alternating with two tunnels, one under the Thimble Shoal Channel and one under the Baltimore Channel. Four artificial islands were built where the tunnels met the bridges.

29 Miles

I watched the bridge-tunnel, a strange sight to me after the quiet sail down the coast, fade into the distance behind me. Soon I was passing the old Kiptopeke Ferry Terminal, built in 1950, seven and a half miles south of Cape Charles City. A long steel pier had been built here, and nine World War II surplus concrete ships had been sunk to protect the terminal from the waters of the bay. The whole scene looked so unattractive that I decided to keep on for Cape Charles, the largest town on the lower Eastern Shore and a busy port. I arrived at three. Beyond the bustling harbor is a small cove where the local watermen keep their boats. Here I tied up and went shopping for groceries and ice, a mission that entailed walking nearly a mile across the dozens of train tracks that separate the harbor from Main Street.

Before I left, I had found a water hose on the dock and decided to replenish my water supply. Also, I had found some sediment in the water tank, and I wanted to flush out the impurities. I opened the pump faucet in the sink to take care of any overflow. Then I blithely went shopping. When I came back, thirty minutes later, I saw Slick Ca'm across the harbor. I was impressed with how pretty she looked, so low and sleek in the water. I walked around the cove. A waterman sitting on one of the pilings watched me approach. "How much water you carry in that little boat?" he asked. "Fifteen gallons," I said. Then I realized why Slick Ca'm sat so low in the water. When I stepped aboard I found she held a hundred gallons—in the bilges and lockers. The floorboards were covered by nearly a foot of water. The sink had not been able to handle the volume. I ran up on the foredeck and yanked the hose out of the intake. "She full?" the fisherman asked. "Very," I said, and began pumping her dry. Perhaps another ten minutes and *Slick Ca'm* would have been on the bottom of the harbor. It took nearly an hour to float her back on her designed water line. All the storage areas underneath the bunks were full of water. Tools, spare parts, and, worst of all, my canned goods were soaking wet. Some of the labels had floated off, and for the rest of the trip I had a number of surprises when opening the unmarked cans.

At five o'clock things were back to normal. I sailed out of Cape Charles to the next creek north, Kings Creek, a fifteen-minute sail in the still-brisk breeze. Two miles up the creek I found a snug anchorage in five feet of water. The creek, like all rivers and creeks on the Eastern Shore, had obviously once been deeper, for the edge of the water was littered with the remains of large boats that could not have entered the creek now.

The temperature was in the eighties, and a warm southerly wind was pushing us from behind. I sat in the cockpit with a drink, quite comfortable in the short-sleeved shirt I was wearing for the first time. Spring, possibly summer, had definitely arrived. The cold and wet of the last two weeks were suddenly forgotten. It was warm enough to have dinner on deck. At nine I went below to sleep, and dreamed of sinking ships and incompetent captains.

Kings Creek to Onancock Creek I stayed in my bunk later than usual and wondered why I felt so let down. There seemed to be several possibilities. Perhaps my lethargy came from passing the halfway mark of my cruise, perhaps from the sudden hot weather, or perhaps from not having taken a bath in nearly a week. The last thought awakened me completely and I dove into the still-frigid water of Kings Creek. Suddenly it seemed a much better day. The skies were clear, and there was the same stiff breeze from the south.

I made coffee and had a leisurely breakfast. At nine I was under way again. I wore a short-sleeved shirt and exchanged my long pants for bermudas. I sailed wing-and-wing all day: mainsail on one side, the genoa poled out on the other. At noon I lashed the tiller and went below to make a sandwich. We jibed anyway, and the mainsheet carried a life jacket overboard. I spent half an hour tacking back and forth, trying to find it. It was bright orange, yet I could find no trace of it. In the four- and five-foot waves it simply never showed up.

Even so, it was a wonderful sail. Once in a while we would surf on top of a large wave, and my portable speedometer would register six and a half knots. I saw only four ships during the thirty-nine-mile run to Onancock Creek, one freighter and three fishing boats, all far on the western horizon. I also got badly sunburned on my legs, arms, and face. I could not see the western shore of the bay. The Chesapeake is at its widest here, nearly thirty miles, yet shoals are many. I could never sail less than half a mile from the Eastern Shore.

At four I entered Onancock Creek. One of the earliest magazine articles about the Eastern Shore (in *Scribner's,* March 1872) had this to say about Onancock: "The gem of the Eastern Shore is the

The Fifteenth Day

harbor of Onancock, a loop or skein of salt coves widening up betwixt straits of green mounds and golden bluffs, and terminating at an exquisite landing, where several creeks pour into the cove between the estates of Virginia planters."

I sailed up to the landing, not so exquisite a hundred years later, where a large sign said that Onancock was the Cobia Capital of the World. I didn't know what a cobia was, but some inquiries around the wharf set me straight: it's a fish. One of my informants offered to drive me to the ice-house, a necessary errand in this warm weather. It would have to be a fast trip, he said, because he was going fishing. You guessed it—for cobia. I still don't know what this fish looks like.

In ten minutes I was back aboard *Slick Ca'm*. I stowed my twenty pounds of ice, cast off, and dropped anchor ten minutes later in a small cove, surrounded by pine trees on one side and a handsome mansion on the other. I was hot and tired from the difficult downwind steering. After a refreshing swim and a late, light supper, I turned in, resolved to get up early enough to visit Tangier Island before heading into the Pocomoke River.

39 Miles

Onancock Creek to Pocomoke River I was up early, and by sunrise I had already finished breakfast. I motored the four miles out of Onancock Creek to the Chesapeake. It was very hazy. Tangier Island, only seven or eight miles from the mouth of the creek, was not visible, although I am sure that on a clear day I could easily have seen its low, marshy outlines. I set the main and genoa, and in a gentle, already warm breeze sailed a compass course toward Tangier. Watts Island passed on my starboard, a lovely, tree-covered island, no longer inhabited.

This and nearby Tangier Island were called Russells Isles by John Smith when he sailed these waters in June 1608. Walter Russell, a surgeon, was one of Smith's companions on the voyage. Tangier has a population of about a thousand; most of its people follow the water. In 1800 the inhabitants numbered seventy-nine, of whom thirty-three were named Crockett, twenty Evans, and thirteen Parks. The proportion of families has not changed much since; although the Pruitts have appeared, the Crocketts still dominate, and the Evans and Parks families are holding their own.

For centuries Tangier was an isolated community of watermen. But electricity and telephone service, and even an airstrip and a schoolhouse, have come to the island. There is regular ferry service to Crisfield, and in the summer many yachtsmen visit the island and meander up and down the narrow, fence-lined streets of its only town, also called Tangier.

At ten I could see the island clearly. By the time I reached the entrance to the channel into Tangier, the wind had died completely. I dropped the sails, motored past a dredge scooping out a deeper ditch, and tied up at the town wharf. I went for a walk through the narrow alleys and no-

The Sixteenth Day

ticed that the once-vaunted white picket fences were being replaced by modern chain-link contraptions. Progress had indeed come to Tangier! There are a few cars on the island, but many of the islanders get around on bicycles, and the teenagers show a preference for motorcycles.

At Chesapeake House, the only hotel on the island, I was given permission to take a shower. It cost a dollar, which seemed a reasonable price to pay for so rare a pleasure. A half hour later I walked back to *Slick Ca'm*, and then motored farther up the channel to the dock of a seafood company, where I bought some ice. On leaving the dock I ran aground, but a crab boat pulled me off the shoal and back into the channel. On my way out of Tangier Channel, I ran aground again a hundred yards from the dredge I had noticed as I came in. Its crew sent a tiny tugboat over and pulled me off. I was glad to be out in the deeper waters of Tangier Sound again.

I had planned to reach Pocomoke Sound by cutting across the shoal between Little Fox and Great Fox islands. This would have saved a half-dozen miles, but having run aground twice in one day already, I did not want to tempt fate any more. I went around Watts Island and the shoal that marks the remains of Little Watts Island, which covered seven acres when a lighthouse was built there in 1832. In 1944 a storm toppled the lighthouse and washed away the island. Nothing remains today but a small buoy marking a shoal.

There still wasn't any breeze. I was becoming tired of using the engine. As I passed the tiny town of Saxis (called Sykes Island before it was connected to the mainland by a causeway) the wind picked up again. With great relief I stopped, stowed the outboard, and hoisted sail again.

The part of Pocomoke Sound beyond Saxis is

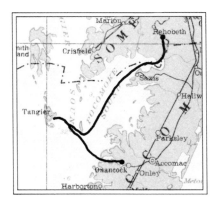

called The Muds. After years of trying to keep the Pocomoke River entrance open, the government finally decided to bypass the problem and dug a new ditch that hugs the northern shore. This channel still has to be dredged periodically, but not as frequently as The Muds, which now is virtually impassable by boats drawing more than a foot and a half. As I crossed Pocomoke Sound to head toward the entrance of the river, I crossed the Maryland-Virginia border, which runs more or less down the middle of the sound and is clearly marked by a series of buoys. The entrance channel also appears to be clearly marked, but I wasn't sure that all the markers were accurate. At least, I ran aground twice. Both times I kedged off in minutes. The grand total of the day's groundings now stood at four—twice in Virginia, twice in Maryland.

At six o'clock I was in the Pocomoke River. I anchored off Shelltown, a tiny hamlet on the north shore, and cooked dinner. But the day had become more beautiful as it wore on, and I couldn't resist going on farther up the river. The haze was gone, and a fresh breeze blew out of the northwest.

The Pocomoke is unusually deep for an Eastern Shore river, and I could sail from one bank to the other without worrying about how much water was beneath me. And the river meanders so much that within minutes I would go from beating, to reaching, to running. The scenery was striking: low marshes at first, and then, a few miles up the river, the first cypress trees began to appear. These are the northernmost stands of cypress in the United States. The water here is not yet fresh, and cypress trees will not grow in salt water. The answer is that the roots of these trees go so deep that they have found fresh water.

At sunset I turned on my running lights. This was the most intriguing sailing I had done, somewhat reminiscent of negotiating the marshes behind the barrier islands but greatly enhanced by the splendid, more varied scenery. When I could no longer see, I reluctantly lowered my sails and carefully set the anchor in the middle of the river, which wasn't more than a hundred yards wide here. I hung the anchor light high in the rigging and hoped that the barges and tugs which use the river didn't travel at night. With the tide changing during the night, I needed room to swing in a circle. I looked at the chart. I was near Rehobeth ("there is room"). I hoped so. I was sound asleep in seconds.

Pocomoke River When I opened the sliding hatch in the morning I thought I was ashore. During the night, after the current reversed itself, I had drifted to within a few feet of several huge cypress trees. If I had let out a few more feet of anchor line the night before, I would indeed have been on land. But it was a morning befitting the Pocomoke—splendid. After breakfast I reread Hulbert Footner's description of the river: "On the river, after passing around the big bend above Rehobeth, the salt marshes disappear for good and the Pocomoke assumes its own unique character. These cypress trees grow nowhere else on the Eastern Shore; the narrow river, lined with dark trees standing in the water, has a tropical quality. It is said to be the deepest river in the world for its width. It has a certain sinister look, but not very sinister; it is too beautiful.

"Yet it changes with the seasons. In spring the dark cypresses are mantled with a fairylike green. I went up in a boat in October and discovered that the trees were not all cypresses; the black river had burst into gorgeous color, the purple and crimson of the gums, orange and yellow ocher of the poplars, scarlet and vermillion of maple and dogwood, the whole picked out with rich green cedar. There are no cutbanks along the Pocomoke to scar its beauty; at high tide no earth at all is visible; the leafage springs directly from the water. When the tide is out, only a few feet of sooty earth is revealed with grotesque cypress knees poking out of the water."

I couldn't wait to sail on. I spent the morning sailing the ten or so miles to Pocomoke City, where the river is crossed by three bridges—first the railroad bridge, then the beautiful bascule bridge that serves the local traffic, and finally the fixed highway bridge, just high enough to allow

The Seventeenth Day

me to pass underneath.

The Pocomoke can be navigated for almost thirty miles to within six miles, as the crow flies, of the waters of Chincoteague Bay. From time to time thought had been given to connecting the two bodies of water, but a growing ecological awareness of the disaster that this mixing of salt and fresh water might produce for the river's vegetation has, fortunately, squashed that idea once and for all.

At noon I approached Pocomoke City. It has gone through a lot of name changes since Colonel William Stevens established a ferry here in the seventeenth century. He called it Stevens Landing. Meeting-House Landing, Warehouse Landing, and, still later, Newtown were all names that were current at different times, and all reflected the activities around what has since 1878 been called Pocomoke City. After passing through the first two bridges, I tied up to the semblance of a dock on the north side of the river. A dapper middle-aged man ran from a small building nearby toward my boat. Once within earshot, I asked if I could tie up for a few minutes while I bought some fresh vegetables. "A few minutes, a few months, a few years—suit yourself. We don't see many sailboats here." I had met another aficionado. Then, in rapid succession, he offered a host of services: Did I need ice? How about fuel? There's a large department store right outside of town. Might he drive me there? I declined with thanks, after expressing my pleasure at all this hospitality. He smiled and answered, "There are no strangers on the docks. When I'm in your port you'll help me out. And this is my port." He owned a little motorboat, he said, but someday wanted to acquire a sailboat. I thanked him again, then stretched my legs walking around Pocomoke City, where I bought fresh fruits and vegetables.

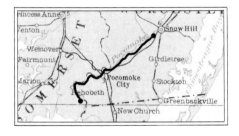

23 Miles

After lunch I continued my delightful sail up the river. The wind changed direction constantly. When it headed me, and forced me to tack, I would sail up to the water lilies bordering both sides of the river and, being careful not to get my mast, sails, or stays entangled in the trees, would come about at the last possible moment, and then head for the other side. The novelty lay in having to look up to decide when to tack, rather than to look to the water's edge ahead.

At midafternoon I lowered the sails and allowed myself to drift into the trees. I tied up to an ancient cypress stump and went for a long, cool swim. The air temperature was hovering around ninety degrees. After my swim I took a nap in the cockpit, the huge trees shading me from the hot sun. I had not yet seen a single boat on the river. Was it always this peaceful, or had I come here just early enough in the season?

I still had several miles to go to reach the end of the river at Snow Hill, but I was already looking forward to sailing back down the river in the morning. An hour later I sailed on. I had heard people complain about the length of the river and the monotony of "poking up the Pocomoke." For me it was like sailing on the Amazon, or on some river in Borneo. As far as I was concerned, this river could go on forever.

3   Toward dusk, just past Shad Landing, I anchored again and made dinner. I opened a choice bottle of wine, which I had been saving for just this kind of a day; having turned over in my mind every one of the seventeen days I had been sailing, I voted this the loveliest yet. After my feast I sailed on toward the bridge at Snow Hill. It was dark now, but there was a full moon, and the wine had made me more intrepid. Snow Hill, settled in 1642, became a port of entry in 1694. This would be the end of the river for me. Actually, it can be navigated with a shallow-draft boat for another two miles on the other side of the bridge, but the part-time bridge tender at Snow Hill requires five hours' notice. I generously decided not to put him to that trouble. Besides, I was getting sleepy.

I turned *Slick Ca'm* around and sailed back down the Pocomoke for a few miles, until I came to what looked in the dark like a promising anchorage. The river here was a bit wider than usual, and several small islands divided the stream in half. Once again I dipped into the river for a last swim. Exuberant, tired, and feeling slightly irresponsible, I finished the last of my prized bottle of wine. The songs that lulled me to sleep were the voices of the loudest frogs I have ever heard.

Pocomoke River to Somers Cove The bullfrogs were still croaking when I awoke. Although rain had been forecast for several days, there was still no sign of it; the skies were clear, and already the sun was pushing the temperatures into the seventies. But there wasn't any breeze at all, and my hope of being able to sail out of the river evaporated. Besides, the tide was flooding, pushing the current against me. I stuck the outboard engine into its well, and for the next six hours *Slick Ca'm* purred her way back toward the mouth of the Pocomoke.

It was Saturday, and at Shad Landing, a handsome Maryland state park with camping and boating facilities, I saw several rowboats from which eager fishermen were trying their luck early in the morning. The bridge at Pocomoke City opened on signal. I was disappointed to be unable to sail out of the river, but I still had a fair amount of territory to cover before time would run out.

Just beyond Rehobeth, where the trees give way to the endless marshes again, I was suddenly face to face—or, rather, bow to bow—with a tugboat pulling a sand barge. The tugboat captain must have seen me first, for his seat in the pilothouse was higher than mine, and my mast would have been visible for miles. My vision was limited by the marsh grass. I quickly got out of his way. And sure enough, at the next bend another tug appeared, this one towing an empty barge. I managed to evade this one, too, and waved at the crew. "Must be nice not to have to work on a weekend," one of them shouted. I wasn't sure whether I agreed or not. Traveling the Pocomoke, weekends or not, couldn't be such a bad job.

These barges were carrying sand to West Point across the Chesapeake, and I gathered that this traffic went on daily, weekend or no. I watched the barges and tugs make their expert turns in the

The Eighteenth Day

river. My respect for their navigational skills increased when I remembered how I, with my shallow draft, had run aground twice at the entrance to the river. And I again scraped the bottom—twice, to tell the truth—around two o'clock, when I entered Pocomoke Sound through the dredged cut. The weather was beginning to change. The tide was turning as I entered the sound, and simultaneously the wind picked up and the sun disappeared behind some low clouds. I optimistically set the genoa jib, but within minutes I hauled it down and replaced it with my working jib. Then I dug out my foul-weather clothes again.

Pocomoke Sound was the site of the first naval battle fought in inland waters of what is now the United States. William Claiborne, an official of the Virginia colony, had established a trading post on Kent Island three years before the first Maryland colonists arrived in 1634. He soon became em-

broiled in a dispute with Maryland's governor, Leonard Calvert. Calvert, in St. Mary's City on the western shore, contended that Kent Island was clearly in his province. Claiborne denied Maryland jurisdiction. Essentially, the dispute was about trading rights: who could sell or buy what, and where. When Claiborne attempted to trade with the Indians on the western shore, the Marylanders confiscated one of his boats. Learning that the Marylanders had sent two pinnaces, the *St. Helen* and the *St. Margaret*, to trade with the Indians on the Eastern Shore, Claiborne sent one of his men, Lieutenant Ratcliff Warren, to make short shrift of the trespassers. The battle took place "in the river of Pocomoque on the Eastern Shore, on the three and twentieth day of April in the yeare of our Lord 1635."

Warren was in command of the shallop *Cockatrice*, and had thirteen men aboard. A shallop is a

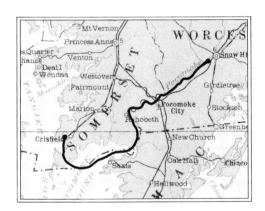

smaller vessel than a pinnace, so Warren was already outnumbered by more than two to one. Captain Thomas Cornwallis, in command of the two pinnaces, gave orders to fire when the *Cockatrice* was within range. She was driven off, and Lieutenant Warren and two of his men died in the fracas. The victors suffered only one fatality.

The dispute about trading rights, ownership, and water boundaries has continued in one form or another down to the present. I was reminded of it when I again passed the carefully placed buoys marking the boundaries of Maryland and Virginia, a precaution on the water that would never have been taken in either state on land.

After a galloping beat across Pocomoke Sound, I reached the entrance to Broad Creek, a narrow canal, partly natural and partly dredged, that would save me twenty miles in getting to the Little Annemessex River and the town of Crisfield, which was my next stop. At five I was in Crisfield harbor and threaded my way into Somers Cove, a small, landlocked basin used mostly by pleasure craft, just beyond the main harbor. Somers Cove boasts a handsome new marina and offers a striking contrast with the disreputable-looking town of Crisfield. Crisfield used to be called Somers Cove, but in 1871, when the town got rich because of a new rail link that speeded northward shipment of its seafood, the grateful citizens rechristened their town with the name of the president of the railroad.

I tied up at the gasoline dock at the marina and headed for the dockmaster's office. "Where can I buy alcohol?" I asked. I had only enough left to cook a few more meals. "Fifths or pints?" he replied with a straight face. I tried to explain about alcohol as a fuel, but he had already decided I was looking for booze and insisted on giving me directions to the nearest liquor store. I finally gave up.

A yachtsman who had overheard the conversation donated a quart of alcohol. When I tried to pay him for it, he laughed and said that the conversation had been worth the price of the fuel. "There are still a number of bootleggers around here," he said. "I was waiting for him to sell you some of his own stuff."

I headed back out of the cove toward the other side of Crisfield, to a manmade waterway called Daugherty Creek, where I had hoped to spend the night. As soon as I entered the canal, the wind died as suddenly as it had started earlier in the afternoon. Simultaneously the mosquitoes came out—in huge swarms. I was in Somerset County now, famous for mosquitoes and mosquito stories. George Carey, in *A Faraway Time and Place*, has recounted many of them in a section of his book called "Remarkable Wildlife." "A Deal Island woman affirmed that a bite by a local mosquito required an immediate blood transfusion. In Southern Somerset County farmers had to put bells on their cows so they could find them after the mosquitoes carried them off. On Smith Island, the mosquitoes began to fornicate with the ducks which upset the hunters and the ecology not a little."

I beat a hasty retreat and returned to Somers Cove—crowded, to be sure, but mosquitoless—where I anchored next to the Coast Guard station. I don't mind mosquitoes, but the swarms in the canal were like one of the plagues of Egypt. I slept with the hatch open, and during the night a wonderful breeze sprang up and kept me swinging slowly around my mooring.

Somers Cove to Webster Cove At seven the next morning I set out for Daugherty Creek again. A gentle breeze from the south pushed me through the narrow waterway and past Janes Island State Park, where a few weekend campers had pitched their tents near the edge of the water. Once we were out in the Big Annemessex River, the wind shifted a little to the east and increased to fifteen knots, a perfect sailing breeze. For the next few hours I sailed toward Wenona, on Deal Island, past the mouth of the Manokin River.

At eleven I sailed through the Lower Thoroughfare into Wenona's harbor and tied up next to a raft of skipjacks. Even on a Sunday there were watermen messing around their boats. In contrast with her reception in other harbors, *Slick Ca'm* did not draw much attention in Wenona. There are more working sailboats—the famous skipjacks—in this harbor than in any other in Maryland, and although my boat didn't really look much like these oyster boats, she was obviously a sailboat.

Deal Island used to be called Devils Island, and the small village not far from Wenona now known as Dames Quarter was called Damned Quarter more than a century ago. Nobody seems to know why and how the names were changed, but perhaps Joshua Thomas, the sailing parson of the islands, who converted many of the people on the Eastern Shore to Methodism, had something to do with it.

I accepted an invitation for lunch (dinner in that part of the world) from Dewey Webster, a retired waterman and the last trailboard carver left on the Shore. Trailboards are the decorative, elaborately carved nameboards tucked up underneath the bowsprits ("splits," the watermen call them) of the skipjacks. I had known Dewey for years, and I had photographed him at work, a privilege he had

The Nineteenth Day

never extended to other photographers. Others were allowed to photograph his work—yes—but not *him* actually at work. When I delivered to him a copy of my book on the oystermen, he gave me a ten-foot-long trailboard that had belonged to the first skipjack I had ever sailed on, the *Caleb W. Jones*. It has hung on my bedroom wall ever since.

We had a combination breakfast-dinner-supper, lovingly and expertly cooked by Mrs. Webster, with seafood dominating the extensive menu, and we talked, as we always did, about the slow demise of the sailing fleet. After the overwhelming meal, and the usual admonition to have "respect for the water," I said good-by and walked across the street back to *Slick Ca'm*. By two o'clock I was under sail again in Tangier Sound.

I wasn't sure where I wanted to go next but decided that exploring the Wicomico River just north of Deal Island would make a pleasant Sunday afternoon sail. A mile or so out of Wenona, the wind picked up and great rain clouds scudded across the sky. I struggled into my foul-weather gear. The rain never materialized, but I got drenched nevertheless by the flying spray that doused me each time *Slick Ca'm* plunged into the waves. I reefed the main and switched to a smaller jib. So much for the weather forecast, which had prophesied variable winds at less than ten miles per hour!

At Sharkfin Shoal, just off Bloodsworth Island, the weather became even rougher. There was a precedent for this. Here Captain John Smith had encountered his first real storm on the bay. "We discovered the winde and waters so much increased with thunder, lightning, and raine, that our mast and sayle blew overbord and such mighty waves overracked us in that small barge that with great labour we kept her from sinking

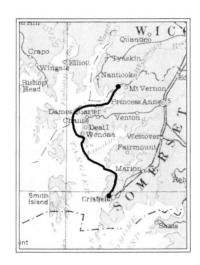

by freeing out the water. Two dayes we were inforced to inhabite these uninhabited Isles which for the extremitie of gusts, thunder, raine, stormes, and ill wether we called Limbo."

I estimated that the wind was now blowing at twenty-five knots; the short, steep seas slowed my progress considerably. Making it into the Wicomico became an unexpected challenge. I stopped thinking about exploring the river; I just wanted to get in it and find some protection.

At six I finally rounded Great Shoals light, at the mouth of the river. It had taken four hours to sail less than ten miles. The water inside the Wicomico was only marginally quieter. I headed for Webster Cove, a miniature basin a few miles up the river on the south shore. Near the cove I dropped the sails and started the engine. The wind was blowing straight out of the fifty-foot-wide dredged channel. Once inside the cove, I moved the gearshift lever to neutral, with no effect; the engine just kept drawing us ahead. Now the only way to stop was to cut power entirely and drift in under my momentum. I narrowly missed several pilings but managed to throw a line around one of them and secure it, and with a shudder *Slick Ca'm* stopped dead in the water, the nylon line stretched to its ultimate elasticity.

I tied *Slick Ca'm* to three other pilings, then began fiddling with the shift lever. As I moved the gearshift lever back, the gears clicked back into neutral and the lever broke off in my hand. There was no way to shift the engine now. An engine that only works in forward isn't so bad, but mine now only worked in neutral. I gave up in disgust.

I walked over to a sort of roadhouse-bar on the other side of the cove and ordered a beer. The two bartenders agreed that the best mechanic lived in the town of Chance, back on Deal Island. In a favorable breeze I could sail there in about two hours. I mulled over the possibility of finishing the journey without power, but time was running out, and I would need the engine to get in and out of some of the places I still wanted to visit. Nothing could be done until morning anyway.

I had a few more beers, went back to my boat, fixed dinner, and looked one more time at the little engine. It was all a mystery to me. I would wait till morning, try to find a mechanic somewhere, and hope that he could fix the engine quickly. The wind had abated at sunset, and the mosquitoes were out in full force. I put a screen in the hatch opening and went to sleep.

Webster Cove to Honga River The roar of a powerful engine woke me. It was already light outside. Seven o'clock; I had overslept again. I removed the screen from the hatch and looked for the source of the noise. A Maryland Marine Police patrol boat berthed on the other side of the cove had started its engines. I hurriedly dressed and walked over. A tall, sandy-haired man in his early forties, with the ruddy face of a waterman but with corporal's stripes sewn on the sleeves of his khaki shirt, emerged from the cabin. C. E. Jones, the name tag on his pocket said. He invited me aboard. "Any problems?" he asked. I told him about my engine. He suggested a mechanic in Princess Anne, thirteen miles up the road. "I'll drive you over there," he said. "The man won't be in until eight-forty. Drives the school bus in the morning." What luck! I also would have a chance to make breakfast.

At eight o'clock Corporal Jones showed up aboard *Slick Ca'm*. I didn't even need to carry the engine. Jones lifted it out of its well and carried it over to his car. By eight-thirty we were in Princess Anne at the mechanic's shop, waiting for the school bus to return. Promptly at eight-forty the mechanic showed up, a gruff and burly man who looked about sixty but was probably younger. He looked at my engine and a few moments later announced with authority that, yes, he could fix it, but, no, he couldn't possibly get to it until later in the day; he had already promised to other people more than he could possibly do. I decided to be patient. Besides, I didn't have any other choice.

Corporal Jones headed back to his patrol boat, but not before arranging to have someone give me a ride back to Webster Cove when the engine was repaired. Everything had been simply and quietly taken care of. And that wasn't all. The mechanic

The Twentieth Day

spoke to a young man who had been listening to our conversation. "Maybe Wallace here will help you out." Wallace, he explained, was very good with mechanical things. Wallace accepted the job, picked my little engine up and put it in the back of his pickup truck. Off we went to his house on the other side of Princess Anne. Wallace Powell, twenty-two years old, skinny and towheaded, worked in the garage of his home. He was the most organized man I had met in a long time. In minutes he had found the source of the problem. His tools were stored in foam-lined cabinets; he could reach for the tool he wanted without looking. After using each one, he'd wipe it clean and replace it in the drawer it had come from, again without looking.

We needed a certain part. A marine-supply dealer in Salisbury was called. Yes, they had the part. Off we went to Salisbury, ten miles north. In half an hour we were back. Wallace fixed the gearshift lever and some other things while he was at it. He insisted on driving me back to Webster Cove—"to make sure it works"—and when we got there, he even carried the engine back to *Slick Ca'm*. Wallace Powell had a sign in his garage that said "Ten dollars per hour. Fifteen if you watch. Twenty if you help." He charged me six. The engine worked perfectly again. Wallace was satisfied. We each had a beer, and then it was time for me to be on my way again. It was not quite noon.

I sailed out of the Wicomico into Tangier Sound, then through Hooper Strait into the Honga River. At Hooper Strait light I passed another sailboat, under sail, the first I had seen in eighteen days. It was a warm and slow sail, but pleasant. From now on I would undoubtedly begin seeing more sailboats; the cruising season had begun.

The *Coast Pilot*, the *Cruising Guide*, and the

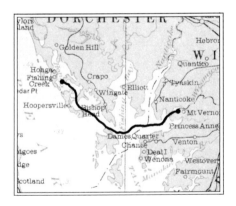

chart all agreed that Back Creek, the harbor of the town of Fishing Creek on Hooper Island, had a controlling depth of seven feet at low tide. In the middle of the channel I ran hard aground in two feet of water. I tried kedging off, but before I could begin winching in the anchor line, a waterman came slowly alongside in his shallow draft workboat. He pulled me off and towed me to the wharf alongside the town, where there was just enough water to float me. "You been lookin' at your map," he said, pointing at my chart. "They ain't right." They surely weren't. I thanked him for his help, then walked to a nearby grocery store to buy some supplies. When I came back the water had risen just enough to allow me to move away from the wharf toward the channel, where, with the centerboard still up, I anchored for the night. I went below to cook dinner.

A few minutes later I heard a splash next to the boat. A young Hooper Islander stuck his head above the water. "How you do," he said. It didn't look as if he were swimming. I had forgotten how shallow it was, and I couldn't see the bottom in the murky water. "Are you standing up?" I asked. "Yeah," he said. "I walked over. Cain't swim." We chatted for a while, then I excused myself to finish preparing my food. The boy walked back across the mud. Beyond the houses on this thin sliver of an island I could see the western shore of the Chesapeake. It was the first time I had seen it since the day I sailed out of the Sassafras more than two weeks ago. I was closing the circle. I reminded myself to get up early, before the next low tide kept me from getting out of this creek and through the channel north of Hooper Island.

Honga River to Sawmill Cove For the second day in a row the sound of an engine awakened me. The fishing boats were leaving Back Creek. It was still dark. I made a mental note to anchor in more secluded places from now on. I turned over and tried to go back to sleep. Then I remembered the tide problem. I quickly dressed, made a pot of coffee, then carefully motored out of Fishing Creek harbor, past Wroten Island, to the bridge at Honga.

The bridge tender was a pro. I didn't even get a chance to blow my horn. Nor did I have to slow down—the bridge was in the right position at the right time. I literally felt my way through the channel, with my centerboard acting as a depth-finder. Once I had to open the engine full throttle to plow through the soft mud. The tide was almost dead low now. I crossed Tar Bay, then blundered through Barren Island Gap. The sun rose as I entered the deep waters of the Chesapeake. I turned off the engine, taking advantage of the southwesterly breeze. I scooted along Taylors Island, then rounded James Island and entered the Little Choptank.

I spent the rest of the morning aimlessly sailing the many creeks. Some I entered, some I sailed past: Slaughter, Fishing, Church, Gray, Beckwith, Phillips, Hudson, Brooks, Lee, Parsons, all within a few miles of each other. I lunched in Madison Bay, then decided I would leave the Little Choptank, sail around to the Choptank, and head for Cambridge. I would just see how far I could get before it got dark. This was too wonderful a breeze to waste.

I sailed past Trippe Bay and, after rounding Cook Point, I was in the Choptank, the longest river on the Eastern Shore. Toward six, I found myself near La Trappe Creek, a few miles below the bridge at Cambridge. It looked like the most

The Twenty-first Day

promising place for a snug anchorage. I sailed into La Trappe, past a perfectly crescent-shaped, white sandy beach, until I reached a tiny cove, a mile or so up the creek. Sawmill Cove was utterly secluded. Two large sailing yachts were anchored at the entrance—they obviously couldn't make it in. I was reminded of the Barrie brothers' advice in *Cruises:* "To thoroughly explore the Chesapeake and its tributaries, one should have a vessel of not more than three feet draught—that is, if one wishes to look into every nook and cranny, to investigate places never seen and for that matter never imagined by the great majority of yachtsmen. Any draught up to ten feet can find good harbors and lots of them, but as the draught increases the limit of ground explorable decreases. With five or six feet one can keep going for some time and never anchor in the same harbor twice." I had the cove to myself. I sailed in as far as I could, right up to the trees at the far end. I never touched bottom. The cove was completely landlocked. I couldn't see the boats at anchor at the entrance. I lowered anchor and went for a swim.

Except for my anxiety about the channel at Honga, this had been a lovely day. I had seen several boats on the Choptank, most of them apparently headed for Oxford. La Trappe Creek, too, with lovely, heavily wooded shores and deep water, had a half-dozen boats anchored inside. I was no longer as alone as I had been. Then I remembered that the coming weekend would be Memorial Day weekend, the traditional start of summertime cruising. Somehow that thought jarred me. I didn't have to be back by Memorial Day, but now I wanted to. I didn't want to spoil the memory of the solitude of these last three weeks. I decided to cut the journey short by a few days and get back before all the hectic activity

47 Miles

started. I wanted to remember the Eastern Shore as I had experienced it this day—peaceful, quiet, and startlingly beautiful. This would give me three more days. After dinner I went for a swim again. I didn't bother to hoist the anchor light. I would be the only occupant of the cove tonight.

Sawmill Cove to Dun Cove I was up an hour before sunrise. Through the trees I could already see the eastern sky begin to lighten. I marveled at this serene spot. It was warm. I dove into the cool water, swam until I got hungry, and then made breakfast. I was washing the dishes by the time the sun came up. I raised the sails, broke out the anchor, and slowly sailed out of the cove. The water was smooth as ice, but the rustle of the trees on the edge of the cove gave a hint of what to expect once I was out of this secret spot. I tacked a dozen times before reaching La Trappe Creek. The big sailboats were still there; nobody was yet up on deck.

Then there came the pleasure of sailing in a strong breeze in close quarters. The creek is so protected here by the trees on its shores that wavelets hardly formed. Once out in the Choptank I had to make a decision. I could go farther up the river, to Cambridge or beyond, or head toward Oxford on the Tred Avon. My new time limit made the decision for me. Oxford, "sitting on the shore with its feet in the water," won out.

At ten I sailed into Town Creek, Oxford's harbor. At one of the marinas I replenished my water tank, bought ice, and found a shower. "Go ahead and use it," the owner said. "I won't charge you none, 'cause there's only cold water. I haven't turned on the heater yet. Might do it tomorrow. Memorial Day coming up." He looked at me to see if I wanted a shower that badly. I did. But it was

The Twenty-second Day

less fun than swimming in Sawmill Cove.

Afterward I sailed up the Tred Avon, almost to Easton. By noon I had seen half a dozen sailboats, and this on a weekday! Summer was upon us. After lunch I sailed back, past Oxford, and beat my way out of the Tred Avon. The humidity was very high, and a haze stretched over the waters of the Choptank. It smelled like a thunderstorm. I sailed on toward Tilghman Island. I had been gone three weeks, and the journey was rapidly coming to an end. The sailboats were proliferating, as were the flies and mosquitoes. I still wanted to sail Eastern Bay and the Wye River and, in order to complete my circumnavigation, sail back around Kent Island.

I turned north into Harris Creek and found an anchorage in Dun Cove, the nearest protected harbor to Tilghman Island. The cove, a favorite rendezvous for weekend sailors in the summer, was still deserted. It also offered decent protection from the northwest and from the thunderstorm, which looked imminent. I could hear a tractor working the fields just beyond the cove.

A puny squall came through at six, but the lightning never came near, and the wind did not amount to much. Unfortunately, the storm did not clear the air. The haze was simply replaced by gray clouds. I dug out my boots from underneath the starboard bunk and laid my yellow slickers out. I had a feeling I was going to need them the next morning.

29 Miles

Dun Cove to Wye River I woke to the sound of rain and the realization that this was my next-to-last day on the Eastern Shore. The rain came down in sheets, but its drumming on the cabin roof sounded rather cozy. I stayed in my sleeping bag for some time. The view through the portholes was not encouraging. The sky was a dirty gray, with no sign of clearing. Static on my AM radio denoted thunderstorms, although none was near.

I took my time about breakfast and the cleaning chores and then decided to brave it. I dressed in my slickers and boots and ventured up on deck. Somehow all the discomfort was stimulating. I motored the few miles to Knapps Narrows, which separates Tilghman Island from the mainland. Visibility was so bad that I had to sail by my compass until I reached the Narrows. I tied up at the bridge and thought I'd while away some time in the island's marine hardware store, waiting for the rain to stop, listening to the watermen who come there to talk and play checkers. I found an excuse to make some purchases; I didn't really need anything. The talk was about crabs, crabbing, boats, and the weather. As Wendell Bradley wrote in *They Live by the Wind*, "Everyone on Tilghman still watches the weather and lives by the wind. When the fire siren blows on a foggy night, it doesn't usually indicate a blaze—it means that a member of the community is still out on the water and his neighbors are concerned about guiding him home. The direction of the wind, its strength, what it did yesterday and what it may do tomorrow are known not only to the men on the water but also to the women in the packing house and to the storekeepers."

The consensus among the men in the store was that it would be quite a while before the rain would stop. I set off through the Narrows and out

The Twenty-third Day

in the Chesapeake again; I stowed the engine and began sailing. The wind was out of the southwest, at fifteen knots, occasionally gusting to twenty. It was perfect for getting me where I wanted to go: through Poplar Island Channel and around Claiborne and Rich Neck into Eastern Bay.

A few crabbers, all wearing the same kind of black slickers, were working their pots. I steered by the compass. My hands were shriveled from the constant exposure to the rain. The crabbers must have wondered what I was doing out on such a day.

At one o'clock I rounded Rich Neck. I had had enough of the rain, and I decided to duck into Tilghman Creek, dry myself out, restore my waterlogged skin to a more normal condition, make a gourmet lunch, and wait for the rain to stop. Even in this weather Tilghman Creek looked inviting. As soon as I dropped the hook, the sun came out, the rain stopped, and my spirits were restored.

At two I sailed across the Miles River to the entrance to the Wye, one of the prettiest rivers on the Eastern Shore. It has a number of branches and innumerable creeks and coves. In the middle of all this water sits Wye Island. I wanted to spend my last evening on the Shore on the Wye. I sailed up the Wye East to Wye Landing, then turned back. Unfortunately, I could not circumnavigate Wye Island, for halfway around it has a fixed bridge with only a ten-foot clearance. I anchored in a small cove off Dividing Creek.

It was still early—five o'clock—but I wanted some time to think about where I had been and what I had seen. I was surrounded by trees on three sides. The fourth quarter gave a view across the Wye. I was so close to the trees of the island that I could easily have tied a mooring line to one of them. The only evidence of humanity here was

a duck blind discreetly tucked away underneath some low branches. The promise for the morning was a clear sky and good breezes. I went for a swim and managed to come to within thirty feet of a blue heron before he saw me and took off with a great flapping of wings. I climbed back aboard, toweled myself dry, finished the last of my vodka, and heated the imported beef Stroganoff I'd been saving.

Tomorrow evening, the beginning of the weekend, this very cove would probably be occupied by several boats, and hundreds of vessels would visit the Wye River. But tonight I was still alone. The news at eight o'clock said that the proposed development of Wye Island had been abandoned by the developer in the face of opposition by the local citizenry. I slept peacefully.

Wye River to Chesapeake Bay I was up before sunrise, for I wanted this to be the longest day. After breakfast I stood in the companionway with a cup of coffee and watched the sun slowly emerge from the multicolored clouds above the river. I had never seen such a spectacular sunrise. I remembered the old saying, "Red sky in the morning, sailor take warning," but the sight was too glorious for the adage to be taken seriously.

I hoisted anchor and sailed out into the Wye East. At Shaw Bay I turned north into the Wye proper and sailed the five miles to the head of navigation. I motored back out into the southerly breeze. Optimistically, I had first put on shorts and a tee shirt, but the weather was turning colder as the sun rose higher, and so I changed into warmer clothing. A half-dozen clammers were working Shaw Bay when I sailed past it again.

As I turned from the Wye into the broad expanse of the Miles River, I could see in the distance, beyond the trees on Kent Island, the towering spans of the Bay Bridge glinting in the sunlight. It seemed very close, but I would still have to go nearly thirty miles. I could sail back via Eastern Bay and Bloody Point, or I could go through Kent Narrows and around Love Point; either way would be the same distance. But all through the journey I had made it a point to go through as many cuts and pass underneath as many bridges as I could, so as to stay closer to the Eastern Shore. Kent Narrows was the logical final choice.

By ten o'clock the promise of the beautiful day had completely evaporated. The breeze increased in strength and changed direction a few degrees toward the north. The sun had completely disappeared. The old weather proverb was being borne out. But I was sailing again and would sail home, come hell or high water. The threatened rain be-

The Twenty-fourth Day

gan to fall, and I hove to and put on my foul-weather gear once more.

Later in the morning, as I approached the bridge at Kent Narrows, the rain, which had been a sort of drizzle, became more violent. It was difficult to see ahead. The *Tidal Current Tables* indicated that I would be going through the Narrows when the ebbing tide was strongest; it often runs in excess of two knots. I got out my Freon-powered horn to signal the bridge tender, but I could only squeeze out one blast before the Freon gave out with a sickening sigh. I dove down below to retrieve my spare canister, but the tender had apparently noticed me and perhaps deduced my predicament. By the time I found the spare can, the bridge was open. The rushing current made it difficult to steer through the narrow opening, and I was glad to reach the other side unscathed.

I plowed on in the rain through the crooked but well-marked channel until I was back in the Chester River, at the exact spot where I had been twenty-four days earlier. At Love Point the rain stopped, but the wind grew stronger yet, and I cranked in a few turns on the roller-reefing boom. The sun came out again, and I gratefully took off my foul-weather clothes for what I thought would be the last time.

The Bay Bridge was now less than five miles ahead. It was an easy beat to the main span. I wasn't going to bother with the other spans, although I could easily have cleared all of them. I felt that *Slick Ca'm* deserved no less than the main channel. She would have 156 feet to spare. Above the bridge a distinct yellow-brown layer of smog was already in evidence. Traffic for the Eastern Shore was on the move. All these people were trying to get to the place I had enjoyed so much in the last three and a half weeks. Summer had be-

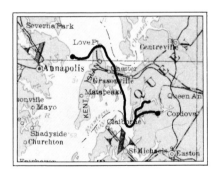

gun, and the Eastern Shore, for the next three months, would not be the same.

At two I crossed my starting point. The journey was over. I had been gone twenty-four days and had covered nearly seven hundred miles, an average of twenty-eight miles a day—very respectable, considering that *Slick Ca'm*'s top speed was a little over five knots. The actual circumference of the Shore is somewhat more than four hundred miles, but I had poked up as many creeks and rivers as time permitted. I could have made the journey faster. If I had had a crew and had used my engine more often when the wind wasn't favorable, I probably could have done it in a week. And if I had attempted to see everything I wanted to see, the voyage would have lasted a lifetime. As it was, I had made some new friends and had seen a lot of beautiful scenery. I had been very cold and very hot. And it seemed that most of the time I had been wet.

But the journey wasn't over yet. On the other side of the Bay Bridge I was hit by a severe thunderstorm. Once again the slickers and boots came out. I lowered all sails, and while rain and hail pelted my boat, I stayed below and let *Slick Ca'm* drift with the force of the wind. In less than half an hour it was all over, and I sailed back into Mill Creek. At five I was back on dry land.

As I squared *Slick Ca'm* away, I thought about all the rivers I hadn't sailed, or hadn't sailed to the end. And about all the towns I hadn't visited and all the creeks and coves and islands I hadn't explored. Someday, I thought, I would love to take a twenty-four-day voyage on the Wye River and find a different anchorage every night. Or sail the Murderkill, Leipsic, Broadkill, or Mispillion rivers on Delaware Bay, all of which can be navigated for some distance. Or sail up Fishing Bay to the Blackwater River, just to see how far I could carry a two-and-a-half-foot draft. Or sail up the Wicomico all the way to Salisbury, a distance of twenty miles. Or up the Nanticoke, navigable to Seaford, Delaware, a distance of thirty-five miles. The Choptank can be sailed for fifty-three miles, all the way to Greensboro. There are thousands of uncharted guts through the marshes behind the barrier islands on the lower Eastern Shore. A shallow-draft boat, a sounding pole, and the patience to wait for the tides could be the ingredients of a wonderful cruise.

I was sad that the voyage was over but happy to be back with my family and friends again. I had lost one life jacket and fifteen pounds. I had sailed some of the greatest cruising waters in the United States. And I had been alone—but never lonely.

Barrie, George, Jr., and Barrie, Robert. *Cruises—Mainly in the Bay of the Chesapeake.* Bryn Mawr, Pa.: Franklin Press, 1909.

Bradley, Wendell P. *They Live by the Wind.* New York: Alfred A. Knopf, 1969.

Brewington, M. V. *Chesapeake Bay, a Pictorial Maritime History.* New York: Bonanza, 1953.

Burgess, Robert H. *Chesapeake Circle.* Cambridge, Md.: Cornell Maritime Press, 1965.

Byron, Gilbert. *Early Explorations of the Chesapeake Bay.* Baltimore: Maryland Historical Society, 1960.

Carey, George C. *A Faraway Time and Place.* Washington, N.Y.: Robert B. Luce, 1971.

de Gast, Robert. *The Oystermen of the Chesapeake.* Camden, Me.: International Marine Publishing Co., 1970.

———. *The Lighthouses of the Chesapeake.* Baltimore: The Johns Hopkins University Press, 1973.

Earle, Swepson. *The Chesapeake Bay Country.* Baltimore: Thomson-Ellis Co., 1923.

Federal Writers' Project, W.P.A. *Maryland, a Guide to the Old Line State.* New York: Oxford University Press, 1940.

———. *Delaware, a Guide to the First State.* New York: Hastings House, 1955.

———. *Virginia, a Guide to the Old Dominion State.* New York: Oxford University Press, 1956.

Footner, Hulbert. *Maryland Main and the Eastern Shore.* New York: Appleton-Century, 1942.

———. *Rivers of the Eastern Shore.* Cambridge, Md.: Tidewater Publishers, 1944.

Gray, Ralph D. *The National Waterway—A History of the C. & D. Canal.* Urbana: University of Illinois Press, 1967.

Hall, Clayton Colman, ed. *Narratives of Early Maryland.* New York: Charles Scribner's Sons, 1910.

Middleton, Arthur Pierce. *Tobacco Coast, a Maritime History of Chesapeake Bay in the Colonial Era.* Newport News, Va.: The Mariners Museum, 1953.

Radoff, Morris L. *The Old Line State.* Baltimore: Historical Record Association, 1956.

Richards, Joe. *Princess–New York.* Indianapolis, Ind.: Bobbs-Merrill, 1956.

Rothrock, J. T. *Vacation Cruising in Chesapeake and Delaware Bays.* Philadelphia: J. B. Lippincott, 1884.

Semmes, Raphael. *Captains and Mariners of Early Maryland.* Baltimore: The Johns Hopkins Press, 1937.

Shannahan, J. H. K. *Tales of Old Maryland.* Baltimore: Meier & Thalheimer, 1907.

Stone, William T., and Blanchard, Fessenden S. *A Cruising Guide to the Chesapeake.* New York: Dodd, Mead, 1973.

Turman, Nora Miller. *The Eastern Shore of Virginia 1603–1964.* Onancock, Va.: Eastern Shore News, 1964.

Vallandigham, Edward Noble. *Delaware and the Eastern Shore.* Philadelphia: J. B. Lippincott, 1922.

Whitelaw, Ralph T. *Virginia's Eastern Shore.* Gloucester, Mass.: Peter Smith, 1968.

Wilstach, Paul. *Tidewater Maryland.* Cambridge, Md.: Tidewater Publishers, 1931.

Wroten, William H., Jr. *Assateague.* Salisbury, Md.: Peninsula Press, 1970.

Suggested Reading

Library of Congress Cataloging in Publication Data

de Gast, Robert, 1936–
    Western wind, eastern shore.

    Bibliography: p.
    1.   Delmarva Peninsula—Description and travel.
2.   Sailing.   3.   de Gast, Robert, 1936–   I.   Title.
F187.E2D43   917.52'1'044   75-10924
ISBN 0-8018-1767-6